The Dy...
Family :

The Dynamics of
Family Business

Building Trust and Resolving Conflict

✦

Kenneth Kaye

with an Introduction by Joseph H. Astrachan

iUniverse, Inc.
New York Lincoln Shanghai

The Dynamics of Family Business
Building Trust and Resolving Conflict

iUniverse books may be ordered through booksellers or by contacting:

iUniverse
2021 Pine Lake Road, Suite 100
Lincoln, NE 68512
www.iuniverse.com
1-800-Authors (1-800-288-4677)

ISBN-13: 978-0-595-35708-6 (pbk)
ISBN-13: 978-0-595-80186-2 (ebk)
ISBN-10: 0-595-35708-3 (pbk)
ISBN-10: 0-595-80186-2 (ebk)

Printed in the United States of America

Contents

Introduction

RESEARCH consistently shows that conflict plays pivotal roles (both productive and destructive) in family and business health and prosperity. Conflict can cause miscommunication, a lack of communication, and an inability to set priorities or resolve crises. Conflict can lead to a loss of employee morale and psychological problems in family members. Yet there has been little research and scant useful theory on the sources and effects of conflict in family business.

Ken Kaye is a pioneer in the understanding of conflict in family business. His writings have affected my work greatly. He has identified and explored the myriad of interactions among elements of conflict, from the role of childhood experience and family pathology to more immediate issues such as salary and dividends. His forays into topics such as the ways family firms tend to sustain problems, or the process of mate selection, are courageous and insightful.

Conflict is at its heart an emotional process, and one needs to understand this to have a prayer of effecting positive change for individuals, families, and businesses. Without understanding the emotional flow of conflict in a system, the best one can offer is palliative care rather than positive change.

One of my favorite of Kaye's sublime notions comes from his 1991 article in *Family Business Review*. He shows how to analyze what people gain from continuing a pattern of conflict, as well as what they fear will happen if they stop. This idea encompasses the complexity of conflict in a system and the reason it is so resistant to intervention. For example, I have often witnessed families who act as if they would have no relationship if not for their conflicts. Kaye goes beyond identifying the pattern, to demystify it and use conflict as an opportunity for growth.

Research on conflict indicates that older, more prosperous business owning families use flexible conflict management styles. For example, avoidance is appropriate if there is no crisis and people are overly emotional, competition is appropriate for capital allocation decisions, and collaboration is essential for long term decisions such as defining a family's values or developing business vision and strategy. Central to all of these mechanisms is family maturity, effective communication, and a sense of perspective; or as one friend said to me, "I tell my clients they have no reason to get excited so long as no one is bleeding or dying!"

1

This book represents a worthy compilation of ground breaking material. Casual as well as serious students of family business should study Kaye's ideas. Future scholars should consider his work as the basis of testable theory. And we should all look forward to Kaye's next work.

Joseph H. Astrachan, Ph.D.
Editor, *Family Business Review*
Director, Cox Family Enterprise Center
Wachovia Eminent Scholar Chair of Family Business
Coles College of Business
Kennesaw State University

Author's Introduction

THE FAMILY ENTERPRISE is the basic form of human organization. For tens of thousands of years, children worked with their parents, brothers labored communally, men and women who married into families took on roles in those families' hunting, gathering, farming, trading, craft workshops—and eventually, stores and factories and merchant banks. Truly, family business relationships are the norm, not an oddity. All human societies are an outgrowth of that biologically determined tendency of humankind.

It was never smooth. From the dawn of human literature we know there were conflicts. The stories of Cain and Abel and of Jacob's sons are about paternal favoritism leading to fraternal violence. Jacob himself was an exploited son-in-law. Socrates was tried, convicted, and executed for counseling the son of Anytus to refuse to follow his father into the tanning business. Lear unwisely entrusted his conglomerate to selfish daughters, with tragic consequences. Half the novels of Dickens, and countless modern novels, plays, and movies, deal with family conflicts over business or inherited wealth.

Although the dynamics of family business conflicts have been subjected to psychological investigation for only two decades, they belong to the broader domain of family systems theory and to the study of organizational development. There is hardly a better field than family business in which to study family systems in their developmental complexity across generations.

Like a music CD, this book alternates heavy pieces with light pieces. The heavier and longer articles are all those I published in the journal *Family Business Review* from its inception through 2004, with the exception of book reviews. I am reviving these articles for three different groups of readers.

For consultants and professional advisors who are familiar with family firms, but only recently oriented to their psychodynamics, these papers present my considered perspective along with those of many other psychologists and family therapists who worked in this domain over the past twenty years.

For mental health practitioners new to the field of family-owned business, as well as developmental psychologists and academic students of family systems, the theories discussed may serve as a bridge into this field.

Finally, for experienced colleagues in the psychodynamics of family business, I hope that rereading these observations and having them accessible in one place will challenge them to disagree, to go deeper, to pose new questions, and even to enrich the science of human development itself, based on the phenomena of families trying to work together from one generation to the next.

I've interspersed those heavy, peer-reviewed articles with a selection from among dozens of shorter pieces I published in magazines over the same period. The ones I chose were aimed at advisors to family firms as well as business owners and family members. Less academic in tone than those in the pages of *Family Business Review*, they summarize some of the main ideas I elaborated in the journal articles. Readers with backgrounds in psychology will find these short articles neither especially original nor controversial, whereas the longer pieces contain much they might dispute.

The articles are arranged chronologically. My earlier career had been as a researcher of parent-child interaction processes (Kaye, 1982) and as a family therapist (Kaye, 1984). When I wrote my first article in this field, I had consulted to fewer than two dozen family businesses. Although that number has increased to about two hundred, in rereading these articles I find little I'd state differently today.

Kaye, K. *The Mental and Social Life of Babies*. Chicago: University of Chicago Press, 1982.

Kaye, K. *Family Rules*. New York: Walker, 1984. Revised edition, St. Martin's, 1990. Republished: iUniverse, 2005.

§

THIS 1991 ARTICLE in *Family Business* magazine summarizes how a therapist looks at the repeating cycle of conflict in a family system. It's a short introduction to the model I elaborated in my first *Family Business Review* article, published that same year.

§

Resolving Conflict*

Getting at the underlying issue can end the vicious cycle of pain that marks family fights.

WHEN SHE HEARD her terminally ill husband and two sons start yet another round of nasty squabbling, Grace Spyros could do little but mutter, "Here we go again." She knew the combatants' habits well enough. Any minor matter could provoke a sudden outburst. After the fighting ended, several days of stony silence would settle upon the household. Then the men would change into their best behavior, which they wore like overly starched shirts. Within days the cycle would begin again.

Traditional methods of conflict resolution assume that people are truly fighting about what they say they are fighting about and that they want to resolve their problems rationally. Family arguments, however, are far more subtle and far less rational. Family members frequently conspire to sustain conflict because it helps them avoid something they fear might be even worse than the devil they know.

Conflicts that mask hidden fears tend to follow a predictable circular pattern (see "Cycle of Conflict" figure): As anxiety builds, family members initiate arguments that distract them from critical issues. The encounters escalate into destructive battles, which create more anxiety. Eventually, tempers cool down. Sooner or later the family's unresolved dilemmas resurface and the cycle begins once again.

The only way to break this vicious pattern is for families to confront the very issues they have diligently avoided. Sometimes they know painfully well what those issues are and merely need a sensitive advisor to help them talk candidly and constructively. Other times families bury their most important problems so deeply that they need a family therapist.

Buried fears can often be identified by asking, "What would happen if…." For example, "What might happen if you weren't fighting about parking places?"

---

*   by permission of the publisher from January/February 1991 *Family Business* magazine, www.familybusinessmagazine.com

"We'd be fighting about something else."

"And what if you didn't fight about anything?"

"Then Dad wouldn't have any reason to yell at us." In the Spyros family[1], son John thought he was making a wisecrack, but his answer did partly explain the group's behavior. I asked the family more "what if" questions, concluding with this one: "What would it feel like if Ted weren't yelling?" The answer was startling. When the gravely ill patriarch yelled at his sons, the family could pretend he was well.

Analyzing a chronic circular conflict can accomplish several things at once. After family members have identified their shared fears, they can begin to isolate the triggers that divert them into unproductive battles. In the Spyros family, the surest trigger was Ted's decision to take a day off from work because he was feeling ill. One son would pick on the other, who would start a shouting match that would escalate until Ted got involved. A lot of angry words were hurled, but no one ever mentioned what was foremost in his mind—grief for a dying father.

Although conflict can hurt a family and ruin a closely held business, it can also create opportunity. The greatest benefit of analyzing the cycle of repeated clashes is that family members learn routinely to ask one another, "What would happen if…?"

Here is how conflict and resolution played out in Ted's family. Doctors told Ted that he'd die within six months after they removed his pancreas. One year later, Ted was still alive, but pain caused the 54-year-old to spend fewer and fewer hours at his business. For years, Ted and Grace worried that their sons would never get along. Now they feared that Ted's illness would somehow make those fears come true.

The two young men invariably argued whenever their father was too ill to work. Ted, who could bellow with the best, would soon be drawn into the argument. The sons had thus resuscitated their tough, vigorous father, if only for a while. If the argument lasted into the evening, the sisters were sure to get involved, telling their brothers to stop acting like babies. This provoked louder shouting. Eventually, Ted would go into a coughing fit, the women would chastise the boys for "goading" their father. And then the arguing would cease. Within a few days, however, sadness and panic stirred the sons to new conflicts.

---

1.   All names throughout this book are, of course, changed, but all families are actual cases.

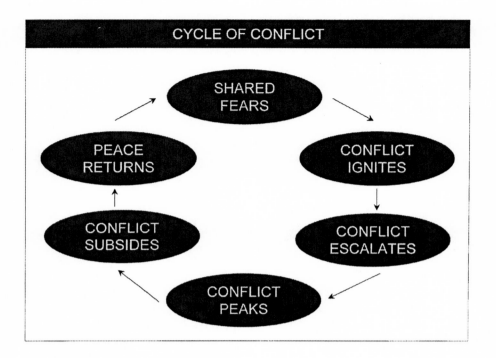

CYCLE OF CONFLICT

SHARED FEARS

CONFLICT IGNITES

CONFLICT ESCALATES

CONFLICT PEAKS

CONFLICT SUBSIDES

PEACE RETURNS

Curiously, the word "death" was taboo in this family. In our meetings, the family referred only to "the situation." I began to explore what might happen if the relatives acknowledged their grief and discussed the problems that lay ahead. I interrupted one of their shouting matches and asked everyone in the room what he or she was feeling. Ted felt "angry." The women felt "aggravated." One son felt "accused," and the other felt "happy because our personalities are finally getting dealt with." I then said I was feeling sad about Ted's prognosis.

I asked, "What might your family be like a year from now if your dad's not around?" After a silence, one daughter replied, "I'm afraid we'll fall apart as a family." She thought that if her two brothers weren't forced to work together, both would distance themselves from the family. The children also feared that their mother wouldn't be able to function without Ted. Grace assured them that she was stronger than they realized.

Only by talking about their deepest concerns was the family able to begin a true healing process. Ted's sons have not become close friends or effective partners, but they finally broke out of their self-destructive patterns and began to talk about the serious matter of what to do with their father's business.

§

IN MY FIRST contribution to the Family Firm Institute's journal *Family Business Review*, I discussed the "problem maintenance cycle," a central concept in the work of William Pinsof at Northwestern University, which I found to be as valuable in addressing family business conflict as it is in family therapy generally.

§

Penetrating the Cycle of Sustained Conflict*

Analysis of a family's chronic cycle of escalating and retreating from conflicts is a powerful tool for breaking the cycle, resolving conflicts, and improving relationships.

CONFLICT RESOLUTION is a special area of concern to those who work in or with family businesses. Conversely, family business issues offer special challenges to both the professional mediator who seeks to resolve and the social scientist who seeks to understand chronic, destructive, or crippling disputes.

The purpose of this article is to suggest how family business consultants can apply a conflict-resolution model that is derived from theories of family and familylike systems. Although the sustained conflict cycle, or "problem maintenance system" (Pinsof, 1995) is the theoretical basis of some techniques used by family therapists, the two specific techniques explained here can be applied by any consultant or by family business members themselves. Toward the end of this article, criteria are suggested for when and how mental health professionals should be involved in consultations with families in conflict.

Orientation

The simplest models of conflict resolution assume that people really are fighting about what they say they are fighting about. This may often be true of disputes between strangers who happen to transgress one another's rights or threaten one

---

*   *Family Business Review,* 1991, Vol. IV, pp. 21-44. Reprinted with permission from the Family Firm Institute, Inc. All rights reserved. This article was first presented to the Dispute Resolution Colloquium at the Kellogg Graduate School of Management, Northwestern University. The author thanks Jeanne Brett, Stephen Goldberg, Mike Henning, Marguerite Millhauser, and Emesto Poza, as well as the anonymous reviewers, for their insightful comments on the first draft.

another's interests, but it is rarely the case between spouses or among relatives or longtime business partners. Furthermore, many approaches to conflict assume that people normally behave rationally: if they behave irrationally, it must be because they do not have adequate information or do not communicate clearly with one another. This article does not make that assumption. Finally, while most models assume that people want to resolve their problems, human beings are actually more interesting than that. Sometimes we only want excuses not to resolve our real problems.

This article makes three claims. Its first proposition is that conflicts *within* organized groups of related or mutually dependent people are fundamentally different from conflicts *between* separate parties. Although kinship or marriage relationships do add extra dimensions to within-group conflicts, the fundamental distinction is between all types of conflict within groups (including, for example, incidents among co-workers) and conflicts between disputants who lack any long-term relationship (as in a product liability suit). Unfortunately, most models of conflict resolution view disputes as arising between clearly separate parties or at interfaces between non-overlapping groups. Therefore, these models are usually inadequate for understanding or helping to resolve conflicts among the members of a closely held firm.

This article's second proposition is that within-group (or within-system) conflicts follow a dynamic pattern. Some features of that pattern are generic; for example, it is usually circular. Nevertheless, each family or family-like group of people creates and sustains conflicts that have their own characteristic sequences, repeated time after time. Analysis of a group's chronic pattern is a vital and powerful tool for resolving its conflicts and improving members' interaction.

The third proposition advanced here is that such conflicts are not merely defensive on the part of each individual against the others. They are also collusively defensive in that the members collaborate—often instinctively and unconsciously—to protect their whole system from something that threatens them even more than conflict with one another does. It often requires an outsider to discern their unspoken, hidden, barely hinted-at apprehensions. Enabling the participants to discuss their real fears is the key to resolving their conflicts because, in most cases, they have been using conflict to forestall coming to terms with those undiscussed issues.

Definitions

We use the word *system* (short for *social system*) for any group of people with some shared history or knowledge of one another's actions and some shared intentions:

people trying to get somewhere together. Thus every family, every business, and every group of two or more co-workers is a system. Human systems are characterized by communication, by rules (norms), and by being *open* (which means that they adapt to changing conditions, including other surrounding and intersecting systems).

Human systems do not often operate the way well-oiled machines do. Conflict is a normal, healthy aspect of all systems. One can easily distinguish, however, between conflict that drives a system toward its objectives, toward constant reevaluation and new objectives, and conflict that mires the system down. This article uses the word *conflict* in the latter sense. When we speak about resolving conflict, we mean getting the truck out of the ditch and onto the road, not shutting off the engine.

Related-Party (or Within-System) Conflict

Negotiation and mediation specialists look for win/win solutions. Some of the techniques used to facilitate win/win solutions apply to related-party and separate-party disputes alike. For example, probably all mediators spend time clarifying the messages exchanged between parties. Another thing we do is to block people from reacting to their own assumptions. We force them to check those assumptions with one another: "I hear you saying _____," "Do you mean _____?" "Is that how you think George would react?" A third tactic, used regardless of whether the parties are related, involves separating the points on which they essentially agree from those that require negotiation. Another is to emphasize the costs of prolonging the dispute, as against the benefits of settlement (Simmel, 1950; Deutsch, 1973; Blake and Mouton, 1984).

Notwithstanding their similarities to other kinds of conflicts, within-group disputes (of which family business disputes are quintessential examples) have some special features that call for special handling. The most important distinguishing feature is that the parties to the dispute cannot walk away from it easily. Separate organizations, or individuals with little relationship to one another, have the option of settling a dispute financially and ending their relationship. That is not a satisfactory solution for parties who must continue to work together or who are related to one another by kinship or marriage. Another feature of conflict within groups is that the parties usually share some long-term goals, which override their separate interests and even override their common material interests. One of those goals may be to strengthen their relationship (Miller and Rice, 1970; Lewin, 1948; Weber, 1947). Moreover, the parties typically hold simultaneous memberships and play roles in several intersecting systems, not just the one in which the lines are drawn for a dispute. This may be true in all kinds of disputes (Coser, 1956), but the likelihood of an individual's identifying with two or more factions is much greater in within-group disputes.

Because family business conflicts have these special features, no matter which members are involved (parent and child, sibling, spouse, in-law, members in the business, members out of the business) and no matter what kinds of issues are at stake (inheritance, management, growth, power, role definitions), family conflicts are never linear problems, with a cause leading directly to an effect, and they are never traceable to one party's behavior. They always turn out to be what we call *circular* or *systemic*. This simply means that the members react to one another's problematic behavior (irresponsibility, aggression, refusal to delegate, withdrawal) in such a way as to maintain, prolong, or exacerbate the very things they are upset about. To make this point clear, let us back up to a simpler model of conflict and see its limitations.

Rational Communications Model

A conflict-resolution model that fits many situations where the parties have no personal relationship with one another (other than their current conflict of interests) is represented by two parties who have to communicate in order to take turns passing over a narrow bridge. The two parties interact only in the sense that they negotiate joint passage, without giving up what is important to them and without forming a permanent relationship. The parties' core needs are compatible; they can accommodate one another once they become willing to be flexible about less important matters. An application might be a dispute between two ranchers over water rights. With good negotiation skills or the help of a good mediator, they may discover that where they had thought there was only room for one of them to succeed, both can do so. This model is based on two assumptions:

ASSUMPTION RC-1. It is primarily inadequate communications that make parties' interests appear incompatible and also make each party react defensively, emotionally, and irrationally. This situation tempts them toward rights-or power-based (win/lose) resolution.

ASSUMPTION RC-2. Rational people revise their behavior when they see better ways to achieve their objectives.

These assumptions lead to a fairly well established approach to resolving conflicts: get both sides to state their priorities clearly, improve their communication so that they can work together to clarify their points of agreement, and negotiate their points of disagreement by means of compromise, trade-offs, and compensations.

Two examples of this approach are Blake and Mouton's (1984) "interface conflict-solving model" and Fisher and Ury's (1981) "reconciling interests" approach. Both seek win/win solutions, as opposed to the win/lose outcomes typical of appeals to rights or the lose/lose outcomes of power-based resolution (for example, warfare). The effort to reconcile mutual interests through rational, constructive communication is often successful, but this model applies only when the parties' ostensibly endorsed interests are more potent than their hidden reasons for maintaining their problem. What can be done about the unarticulated, the unconscious, the unacknowledged?

Rational Interactions Model

A more realistic model of conflict between parties who have any kind of relationship with one another—even a brief one—is shown in Figure 1. Instead of picturing two or more parties with independent intentions that may or may not be compatible, this model acknowledges that people trigger one another's behavior and interact as a system. In fact, their perceptions, beliefs, and attitudes interact, and each of these is affected by the other person's behavior and, in turn, shapes the perceiver's own subsequent actions (Bateson, 1972; Coser, 1956; Deutsch, 1973). **A** responds to his or her perception of **B**'s intentions in a fashion that elicits a response from **B** that is very likely to confirm **A**'s perception. **B**'s behavior is partly an outgrowth of **B**'s perception of **A**'s intentions. Each party's defensive or pre-emptive maneuvers are perceived as offensive by the other. Thus each participates circularly in maintaining and escalating the conflict while blaming the other. As Figure 1 indicates, the fact that **A** and **B** comprise an interacting system creates the risk of their escalating to a lose/lose conflict. (The twenty-five-year arms race between the United States and the Soviet Union was a classic example of such risk; other illustrations can be found in such places as Northern Ireland and the Persian Gulf.)

The sensitivity of **A** and **B** to one another's behavior also has a promising aspect, however. It implies the possibility of change, so that they can learn to coordinate their efforts toward common or mutual goals (win/win). Unfortunately, in the absence of a mediator, both parties are usually afraid to lower their defenses.

What assumptions does this model make?

ASSUMPTION RI-1. Rational people revise their behavior when they realize it is counterproductive (same as RC-2).

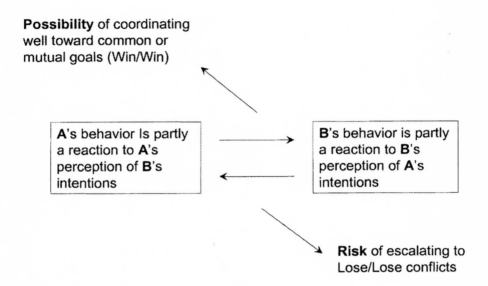

Possibility of coordinating
well toward common or
mutual goals (Win/Win)

| A's behavior Is partly a reaction to **A**'s perception of **B**'s intentions | B's behavior is partly a reaction to **B**'s perception of **A**'s intentions |

Risk of escalating to
Lose/Lose conflicts

ASSUMPTION RI-2. Insights about their interaction system help the parties commu-
    nicate more constructively in the future. In fact, conflicts are not resolved in
    any lasting way unless the system of interaction changes.

When Blake and Mouton (1984) focus their clients on improving mutual understanding so as to avoid similar disputes in the future, and when Ury, Brett, and
Goldberg (1988) help their clients design systems to cut the time and other costs of
inevitable conflicts, they move beyond reconciling clients' interests in specific disputes. They are leading their clients' systems to change.

To the standard "clarify and compromise" approach, the rational interactions
model adds some techniques that are widely used in family therapy. In addition to
improving communication, the mediator points out to each side how it has been
contributing to the problem. By checking their perceptions of one another's intentions, taking responsibility for clarifying their own intentions, and learning to trust
one another, the parties work their way free of an "arms race" type of escalating
loop. A therapist or other professional consultant tries to build up the system's own
capacity to coordinate adaptively and resolve future conflict earlier, with less tur-
moil.

This model is much more sensitive than the rational communications model to
the fact that conflicts arise through interaction. Thus, when applied to families,
work groups, or any other organization, the rational interactions model holds that
for conflict to be resolved, the system of interaction must change.

Nevertheless, this model is superficial. It offers little guidance on the specific aspects of the system's interaction that a change agent ought to focus on. In fact, the model has two weaknesses.

The first weakness is that it does not explain why conflicts sometimes escalate and sometimes deescalate spontaneously. What determines the direction of a particular conflict, in the absence of intervention? (See Figure 1.) In the same way that an understanding of the human circulatory system's disease processes and health-restoring processes gives medical scientists clues to the design of treatments, an understanding of social systems' natural processes of breakdown and restoration would provide crucial clues for the design of interpersonal interventions. (A few researchers actually are studying interaction processes in business negotiations; see Putnam, 1985.) The second weakness is that this model does not necessarily probe beneath the surface of the disputants' conscious, expressed motives. A better model expands this one, at the price of greater complexity but with the benefit of more power to explain and change conflictual behavior when it arises within a set of relationships.

Sustained Conflict Cycle (Equilibration) Model

All family conflicts follow habitual patterns. To know a family's unique pattern of conflict is to know its members so intimately as to be able to predict their crises. This is possible because conflict is not something that happens to them; it is something they suffer to sustain because it serves some function in their system. One of our first tasks is to figure out, in each case, what that function may be.

A way of analyzing conflict in any system and then changing the system could be called the *sustained conflict model.* Unlike the notion of a family system (a useful metaphor, but not an explanatory theory; see Kaye, 1985), this model yields testable hypotheses about conflict in family systems, as well as practical procedures. It is founded on three assumptions:

ASSUMPTION SC-1. Individual members collaborate to sustain the conflict, at a comfortable equilibrium between too much conflict and too little.

ASSUMPTION SC-2. When a conflict grows too intense, it raises members' anxiety about the destructive effects, and this anxiety motivates them to cool down.

ASSUMPTION SC-3. The strange-sounding idea of "too little" conflict is explained by shared fear: as conflict cools, its absence is alarming because it raises members' anxieties about deeper, more catastrophic possibilities. ("I don't like it," says the Hollywood cowboy, cop, or soldier, "it's too quiet.") Those anxieties trigger defensive mutual offenses, which, if they do nothing else, serve to distract the whole system from whatever significant challenge or tough issue or painful acknowledgment it really ought to be addressing.

This conflict-resolution model incorporates the rational communications and rational interactions models already described, but it adds the concept of equilibration. At the center of this model are the major combatants (see Figure 2). **A**'s and **B**'s interaction system undergoes a natural cycle, between too much and too little conflict.

The downward arrows on the right side of this cycle correspond to the one toward the lower right of Figure 1, escalating the conflict to the brink of Armageddon. The upward arrows on the left side of the cycle show the members, of their own accord, defusing their conflict. That portion of Figure 2 corresponds to the upper left of Figure 1: the possibility of coordinating better. In other words, the sustained conflict cycle model hypothesizes that both escalation and de-escalation occur naturally—in each case, just until the level of conflict deviates too much from those levels of sustained conflict at which the system is used to functioning (Bateson, 1972). The key task for a consultant, therefore, is to support the intrinsic processes that are constructive (those on the left side of Figure 2) and then dis- abuse the members of whatever expectations have led them in the past to renew their conflicts. That task is what leads us to probe their shared fear. This article postulates, as a testable hypothesis, that when people who should have common cause appear to be mired irrationally in win/ lose or even lose/lose conflicts, they are often acting in concert to avoid another outcome, perhaps only dimly or even unconsciously imagined, that scares them more than the apparent costs of their fighting.

How can the absence of conflict raise apprehensions? What might those awesome apprehensions (shared fears) be? Some possibilities are listed in the top box of Figure 2. One is loss of family contact: isolation, loneliness, death. Another may be simply the fear of change, of the unknown. Family members may fear (probably correctly) that, in order to address issues about the future, it will be necessary to broach some subjects that they traditionally have treated as taboo, or perhaps they fear that candor may engender intimacy and violate walls that they built long ago around certain emotions. Sometimes skeletons rattle in closets, or long-buried hurts may reemerge. The sustained conflict model suggests that some

Figure 2. Sustained conflict cycle
between individuals A and B

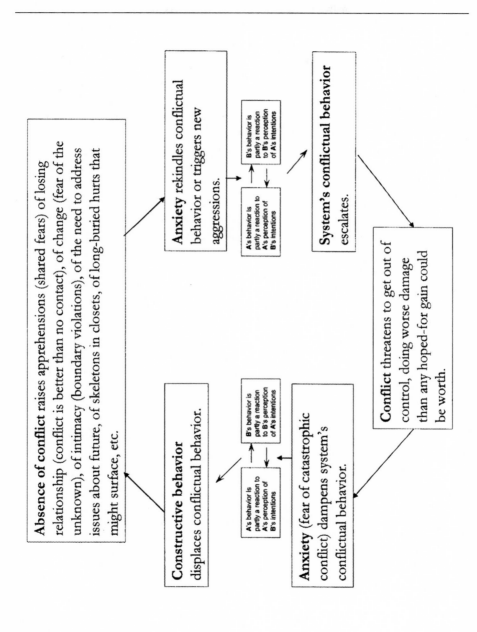

such apprehensions lie at the root of group members' having maintained their conflict over a long period. This is a special application of Pinsof's (1995) "problem maintenance cycle" (a model that applies to a variety of family problems, including, for example, sexual dysfunction in marriage or children's failure in school).

Why would family members behave so irrationally as to sustain their conflict indefinitely? The answer is their shared, almost conscious concern that if the problematic behavior were to stop, a worse catastrophe of some sort might ensue: Dad would have a heart attack, or the sisters would never speak to one another again, or the business would not stay in the family. An effective way to resolve these conflicts involves tracing the problematic cycle of family interaction and elucidating the shared anxieties that underlie it, and then enabling family members to put their apprehensions on the table, where they can be examined and weighed realistically, usually for the first time.

The major combatants are also surrounded by other family members, managers, and shareholders, who all contribute negative and positive feedback (see Figure 3). Charting a conflict, as in Figure 3, can provide outside consultants or even executives themselves with the keys to unlock the cycle and create opportunities for more constructive interactions.

These two major concepts—the sustained conflict cycle, and the idea of shared fear—lead to the following method of conflict resolution:

1. Form an alliance with the system, validating (or "normalizing") its members' fears and resistance to change. For example, a consultant says, "You're quite right to be concerned about that. It's a risk to be guarded against."

2. Call attention to the positive behavior already present (indicated by arrows in the left half of Figure 3). This action reinforces the system members' confidence in their ability to replace conflict with constructive communication.

3. Encourage reality testing and cost-benefit analysis regarding shared fears, correct or incorrect perceptions, and maladaptive behavior (indicated by arrows on the right side of Figure 3).

Figure 3. Sustained conflict cycle supported by others

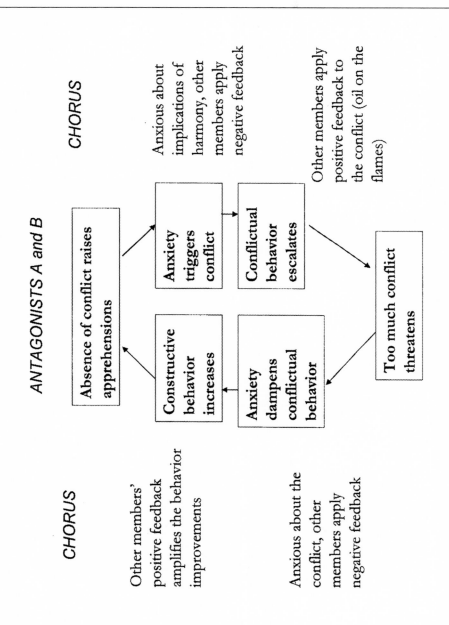

How does one do that? One does not make a frontal assault ("Why do you behave that way?" "What are you afraid of?"); rather, one poses a tactful surrogate question ("What would happen if...."): "What do you think might happen if George reported directly to Sally?" "What might your father's reaction be if you were to tell him that's the way you feel?" "What if we were to put that topic on the table for discussion?" "What would you guess we might be talking about today if you *hadn't* got into that 'big to-do over nothing'?"

Asking for a concrete (although speculative) prediction is invariably more effective than requesting an interpretive analysis of whatever block stands in the way of members' adopting the consultant's suggestions. The individual's prediction turns out to be the very "catastrophic expectation" (Pinsof, 1995) that, untested, has led him or her to persevere in problematic behavior or to avoid a constructive solution. Furthermore, it is often a shared catastrophic expectation, coinciding at least partially with other system members' apprehensions. Thus the consultant must use "What if" questions with one individual after another, comparing expectations and encouraging members to check their assumptions about one another's expectations: "What do you think might happen if George reported directly to Sally?" (Answer: "She would....") "Have you ever discussed that possibility with George or Sally?" ("No.") "What do you think they'd say?" Note that this can be done recursively—"what if " in response to the answer to a "what if," in response to the answer to a "what if," almost ad infinitum. As a result, system members not only see new options for constructive action but also begin to incorporate this way of questioning themselves in their routine discourse.

Table 1 summarizes those features of within-group or "family" conflicts that have implications for resolution facilitators. Some of the indicated intervention techniques fall properly within the professional field of family therapy; others, however, are useful, safe, and often indispensable techniques for any consultant or problem-solving leader. The two cases that will be discussed in the remainder of this article benefited from the tracing of sustained conflict cycles and the elucidation of shared fear. In the first case, it was important that the present author is a licensed psychologist and family therapist. In the second case, that was not important.

Application by Family Therapists

A mental health professional, as distinct from a legal, managerial, or financial professional, emphasizes emotion, the unconscious, personal history, and biological considerations whenever they are relevant. He or she sensitively pursues intimate,

Table 1. Features of Family Conflicts

Characteristics of Conflicts[a]	Implications for Resolution[b]
Some shared goals	Must find, clarify, gain parties' explicit commitment
Negative expectations and distrust are partly communication problems	Discourage assumptions, constantly check parties' mutual understanding, encourage reality testing
Negative expectations based on experience interacting with one another	Chart historical sequence of mutual reactions, showing discrepancies between each party's intentions and others' perceptions
Overt conflict masks unspoken fears	Explore fears realistically
Members use special lingo	Learn it; sense which of their expressions to use, which not
Bonds draw members together despite negative feelings	Members like helper to join all equally (e.g., father who can't stand his son is relieved to hear that mediator likes the son)
Cannot settle financially and walk away	Emphasize human as well as financial costs of prolonged conflict
People belong to several intersecting subsystems	*"Reframe" (constructively redefine) members' goals and contributions, as well as previous conflictual behavior*
Intrinsic cycle of conflict escalation, de-escalation, re-escalation	*Reinforce system's own existing routines for de-escalation*
Same old conflicts are repeated regularly ("Here we go again")	*Coach members to recognize and interrupt destructive patterns*
Courtesies performed with strangers are omitted in family	*Coach people to treat one another like important customers*
Personality, mental and emotional health are factors in any conflict; *families especially stir childhood issues*	*Guide parties to appropriate therapies (family, marital, individual, medical, recovery support)*

a italics = particularly true of "family" or within-group conflicts; other characteristics apply to any conflict	*b* italics = family therapist interventions; other suggestions are for any mediator

perhaps traumatic, aspects of a family's past, if those experiences bear on its members' assessment of present and future reality. Yet the approach discussed here is problem-centered, which means that we solve the problem, if possible, in the here-and-now, and in specific steps that our clients can take in the future. In that respect, we are like other consultants, but we are also prepared to move back to the past and down into the intra-psychic level of experience, as far as necessary. Clarification of shared fear is one of the tools with which we can move to those deeper levels. I shall now illustrate the analysis of a sustained conflict cycle in a family business with which I was involved primarily as a therapist. (All clients' names throughout this article are pseudonyms.)

Ted Spyros, after losing his pancreas to cancer, had been told that he would probably die within six months. Ted was still alive a year later, but his hours at his wholesale food business were restricted by frequent pain from gastrointestinal complications that he was not healthy enough for surgery to correct. Ted and his wife, Grace, were a strong, loving couple with unshaken religious faith. They had two reasons for seeking my help. One was their twin sons' arguing with one another and with Ted. The aggravation that this arguing caused not only reduced Ted's ability to manage his physical pain, it also made Ted doubt his sons' ability to manage the business. The couple's other reason for seeking help, which emerged after several sessions, was concern about the future of all four children after Ted's death.

This was a close family, in the worst sense (see Figure 4). Family members fought with one another every time they met—especially the twins, John and Jimmy, thirty-one, who worked together. All four children, unmarried, were in touch with their mother every day and with their father several times each week. The elder daughter, Peggy, thirty-three, was a schoolteacher, extensively involved with her students' extracurricular activities (chaperoning trips to Europe, directing musicals); her schedule permitted no time for dating. By the norms of her Greek-American heritage, she should already have been married ten years before. The younger daughter, Tammy, twenty-nine, had once been a beauty but was now obese, depressed, and unemployed. She and Jimmy still lived in their parents' home. The parents worried about the younger daughter's apparent destiny as a spinster even more than they did about her older sister's (Peggy, at least, enjoyed some professional success). Ted and Grace worried that their daughters would never marry and that their sons would never get along. They feared that the impact of Ted's illness was cementing those dire fates.

Figure 4. Spyros family.

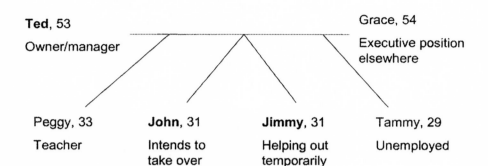

Ted, 53

Owner/manager

Grace, 54

Executive position
elsewhere

Peggy, 33

Teacher

John, 31

Intends to
take over

Jimmy, 31

Helping out
temporarily

Tammy, 29

Unemployed

John's and Jimmy's fighting was a sustained conflict. To all appearances, the twin brothers were enemies, yet they never really did anything to hurt one another except to disagree and argue, as Ted put it, "until who yells loudest." Ted himself was an arguer from way back. In one of our meetings, Peggy complained, "You do it, too, Dad. Before you got sick, you'd argue with them until you were blue in the face."

"Well," Ted said, "maybe I would at one time, but I don't have the stamina for it now. I just get angry and walk away."

The men's arguments followed a clear cycle (see Figure 5). Whenever Ted had had a bad night and did not come to the office in the morning, one of the two brothers would criticize the other, and a volatile argument would ensue. Ted would be drawn into the argument, either by telephone or later, when he came to work. He sometimes took sides in the brothers' dispute but more often staked out his own position, always emphasizing his views by yelling at the son or sons with whom he disagreed. If the argument lasted into the evening or the weekend, one or both sisters was sure to get into the act, telling the brothers to stop acting like babies. This action would provoke louder shouting. Eventually, Ted would go into a coughing fit, one or all of the women would chastise the brothers for "goading" him, and the argument would be dropped—unresolved.

Figure 5. Conflict cycle in the Spyros family.

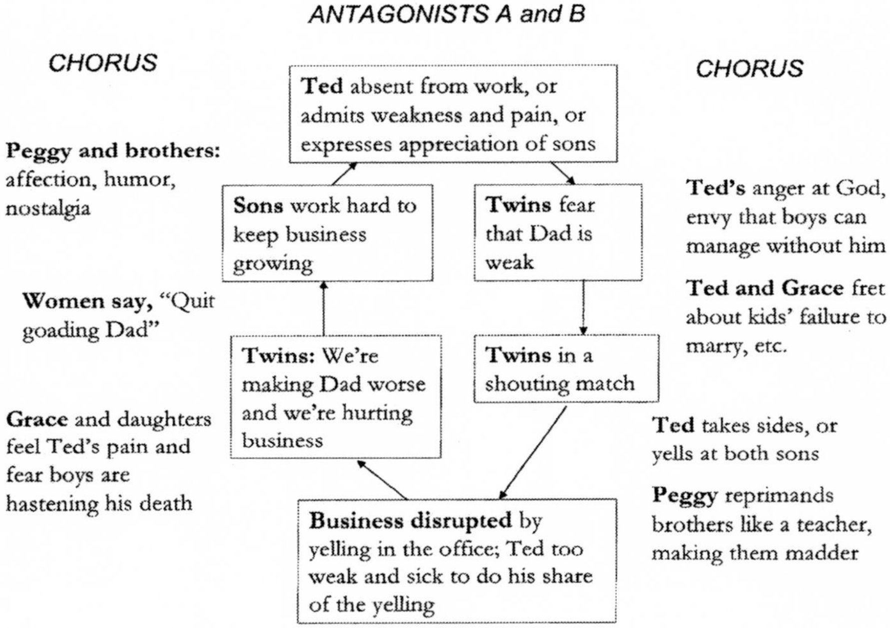

ANTAGONISTS A and B

CHORUS   CHORUS

Peggy and brothers:
affection, humor,
nostalgia

Ted absent from work, or
admits weakness and pain, or
expresses appreciation of sons

Sons work hard to keep business growing

Twins fear that Dad is weak

Ted's anger at God, envy that boys can manage without him

Women say, "Quit goading Dad"

Twins: We're making Dad worse and we're hurting business

Twins in a shouting match

Ted and Grace fret about kids' failure to marry, etc.

Grace and daughters feel Ted's pain and fear boys are hastening his death

Business disrupted by yelling in the office; Ted too weak and sick to do his share of the yelling

Ted takes sides, or yells at both sons

Peggy reprimands brothers like a teacher, making them madder

A comparison of Figure 5 with Figure 3 shows how simple it is to apply the present method to a particular conflict. As in a crossword puzzle, one starts by filling in the obvious or easiest cells: perhaps what the conflict is like at its worst point, or how it seems to start. The intermediate steps in the cycle soon come to light: What does this lead to? What usually provokes that?

Diagramming the Spyros brothers' conflict cycle (Figure 5) made several things clear, first to me and then to the family members. First, whenever Ted's physical condition became obvious, the whole family collaborated to draw him into an argument. He then reacted as the tough, vigorous dad they had known all their lives. For a short time, they could deny the inevitable. Then, after the fight had escalated too far for Ted to win by out-yelling his sons, his wife and his daughters would attack the twins, who would leave each other alone for a while. Soon, however, the very fact that their father was too sick to function as his old self must have stirred sadness and panic in John and Jimmy, and the cycle repeated itself.

Also shown in Figure 5 is another observation: in my meetings with the family, whenever Ted alluded to his illness, and especially when he expressed love, gratitude, or praise for his sons' hard work in the business, his sons attacked him. In one session, for example, Ted told me, "These guys have done a heckuva job coming in under the circumstances."

Jimmy said, "How come you never tell us that?"

"I've told you that," Ted protested.

"No, you haven't," Jimmy said. "I don't recall you ever saying that."

"That's not the point, Dad," John interjected.

Ted ignored John and replied to Jimmy in a calm, sincerely caring voice that apparently clashed with the sons' and daughters' memories of the tough guy he used to be. "Well, if I didn't say it so you heard it, I apologize. I especially appreciate what you've done, Jimmy, because you only came to work because of the situation that exists. I know you wouldn't be there if I were pulling my weight, and I appreciate that."

"We've totally gone off the point," said John, while Jimmy muttered in imitation of their father, criticizing and bossing everyone around in a gruff voice exactly opposite to the voice that had offered the warm, sincere praise I had just heard. Jimmy's mocking performance was accompanied by menacing body language, which seemed quite unlikely to have been produced recently by the frail, prematurely aged father slumped on the couch in front of me.

Another thing apparent in Figure 5, by its omission, is that uttering the words *cancer* and *death* seemed almost taboo as far as the younger generation was concerned. Ted and Grace used those words when they met with me privately. In our meetings with their children, however, they referred only to "the situation" and "the circumstances." The adult children knew the truth—that Ted had no expectation of living until Christmas—but all their references to his health were of the "How are you feeling today?" variety. In fact, they goaded him not to be so gloomy about his pain. At one point, the following remarkable exchange took place:

> JIMMY: All right, you had a bad night, you were up a lot last night, so you didn't feel well, and you didn't come in this morning. You'll be better tomorrow.
> TED: How do *you* know?
> JOHN: How do you *not* know?
> GRACE: When Dad isn't feeling well, I don't think he should be goaded.
> JOHN: Ma, I don't think I'm goading anyone. I'm trying to run a business.
> [John changed the subject.]

The family acted as if our meetings were about anything but death, yet that was precisely what they were about: the sons were fighting to drive away the Angel of Death.

Having formed a mental picture something like Figure 5, I began to explore what might happen if the family members were to acknowledge their grief and discuss the problems that lay ahead. I interrupted one of their shouting matches and asked everyone around the room what he or she was feeling. Ted felt "angry." All three women felt "aggravated." Jimmy felt "accused," and John felt "happy—because all these arguments and our personalities are finally getting dealt with." I then said I was feeling sad about Ted's prognosis and surprised that none of them was aware of feeling that.

"I wonder," I said, "whether maybe it's easier to argue over day-to-day irritations than to think about the future"—a textbook line (we therapists do not try to be original, just effective). And this was effective. The family members indicated, by their expressions more than by their words, that they were ready to be led gently to the point.

I asked, "What might your family be like a year from now, or whenever, if Dad's not around?"

Peggy said, "I'm afraid we'll fall apart as a family."

She thought that if her two brothers were not forced to work together, both would distance themselves from the family. Furthermore, she thought that none of the four adult children had enough in common with the others to sustain a relationship, were it not for the parents' role as a central exchange. Thus it was not Ted's death alone but also the confrontation it forced with aging and the loss of the parents' generation (and, in fact, the young people's own acceptance of adulthood) that, for Peggy, was the real underlying issue. This feeling was shared, to varying degrees, by other family members. (John voiced a different version of the fear: "Ma will fall apart.")

Putting those fears on the table gave family members the opportunity to confirm or disconfirm them. In fact, the children's fears that their mother would break down and their family would fall apart were unrealistic. Grace was a pragmatic, capable person. An office manager for a large check clearing firm, she managed seventy-five employees, about five times the number who worked for her husband and her sons. It reassured her children immensely to hear her say that her life was not over at fifty-four.

After Ted's death, John and Jimmy did not become close friends or effective business partners, but they did break out of their habitual cycle, and they began to talk about more serious matters. Jimmy pursued his own career, while continuing to live with Grace and Tammy, and John arranged to purchase the business from Grace, at an appraised price, over a period of years.

Application by Other Consultants

One need not be a therapist, or even an industrial or organizational psychologist, to analyze a sustained conflict cycle or to use "what if" questions. In some cases, I would argue, the work I do could just as well be done by a financial or a legal consultant who took a few minutes to analyze the sustained conflict cycle. In the case just discussed, I showed the family members their cycle (Figure 5) as an entree into discussing their grief and the younger generation's fears. Everything I did up to that point, including charting and the "what if" questions, would have been equally appropriate for any consultant to do. The transition to the work on emotional relationships could have been handled through a referral to a family therapist. This is an important point because nontherapist consultants do encounter cases where these two techniques are sufficient to get on with the job, and where a family therapist is either not needed or not what family members want. It would be a mistake to hesitate in using these techniques for fear of where they could lead. The place to draw the line between the work of a business consultant and that of a therapist is *after* the analysis of a cycle of sustained conflict.

Flanagan & Sons, an electrical contracting firm, worked primarily on new and rehabilitated office buildings, hotels, and factories. Tom Flanagan had founded the company twelve years earlier, at forty-nine. Before that, Tom had been in the field for thirty years. His last job, before he started his own business, had been as a project supervisor for a much larger contractor. His first employee had been his twenty-one-year-old son Bill, already an experienced electrician with a union card. The company's annual revenues had grown steadily, to about $2 million.

At the time they engaged me as a consultant, Flanagan & Sons' principal employees and noninvolved family members were as shown in Figure 6. Bill, now thirty-three, had left the firm more than a year earlier. Mickey, the principal nonfamily member, had worked for Tom nearly ten years. Sons Tom Jr. and Patrick had both joined the firm about four years before. Daughter Kathy, an attorney with a large law firm, did much of the family business's legal work.

Figure 6. Flanagan family.

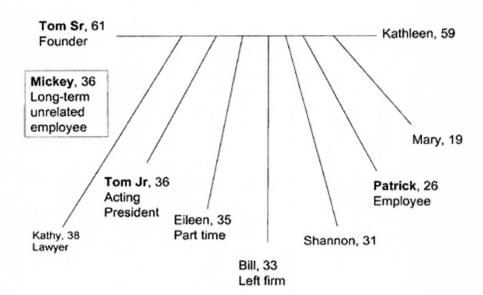

A succession plan for Flanagan & Sons was already in place, and it was the principal underlying problem. Mickey, Tom Jr., and Patrick had signed contracts with Tom Flanagan to buy 74 percent of his stock, in equal shares, over a three-year period. Because there were no other stockholders, Tom would retain 26 percent ownership, and each of the younger men would eventually own a little less than 25 percent. (Originally, their shares had been smaller because Bill had been part of the plan.) To enable Mickey, Tom Jr., and Patrick to buy Tom's stock, the company was paying them $75,000 each in annual bonuses for those three years.

Bill had quit in anger over this take-it-or-leave-it succession plan. He did not like the inclusion of Mickey as an equal partner with the three brothers; in any case, he felt the plan was unsound. Their father viewed it as a gift, "buying himself out" of the business, but Bill saw it as Tom's bleeding the business dry and only then turning over what was left.

Tom Jr. had a different complaint. Ten months into the plan, his father had moved to Florida and left the business in his charge, only to return three months later in an emergency. That emergency—a fistfight in the office—had been created deliberately by Patrick (in Tom Jr.'s view). Tom Jr., the eldest son, was ten years older than Patrick but had no more seniority in the company. For several years after his dishonorable discharge from the Army, for drug use, Tom Jr. had not communicated with anyone in the family. Eventually, he went through a successful recovery program, married a woman with three children, and fathered three more. He and his wife were ardent participants in Alcoholics Anonymous and Al-Anon.

The incident that triggered Tom's return from Florida was repeated several months later in another incident between the two brothers. This was the one that led the Flanagans to seek a consultant. In both cases, Patrick and Tom Jr. had come to blows, but both incidents fit a pattern that had occurred frequently, with less physical violence (see Figure 7): whenever Tom Jr. took on significant administrative responsibility—"stopped working with the tools," as they put it—Patrick resented his brother's assumption of authority. Tom Jr. criticized Patrick for leaving "early"—at 4:30 P.M., when the other wage-earning employees went home. Patrick took offense (or Tom Jr. took offense at his younger brother's reply), and verbal jabs, if not punches, were thrown back and forth until Tom Jr., who had inherited his father's temper, would do something hotheaded that Mickey or Patrick could report to the father.

The next step was that Tom would demote his son back to "working with the tools." Tom Jr. would then have to prove himself reliable all over again, and another target date would be set for the father's departure to Florida. Twice in the past year, Tom Jr. had quit for a week or two before coming back, at his mother's and his wife's urging, to accept his demotion.

When I first met with him, and then with his father, Tom Jr. had left abruptly once again. This time, however, his dissatisfaction with the terms of the buyout contract he had signed was complicating the situation. He had read it carefully and realized for the first time that if he quit, the stock he had "purchased" from his father to date would simply remain in limbo while Patrick and Mickey continued to acquire the rest. Since neither they nor the company would have to buy it back from him, he had nothing with which to start a business of his own. Furthermore, he believed that he had paid income tax on the $75,000 bonus (actually, the tax had been withheld before the stock-purchase payment). In any case, if he quit, he would have no compensation in the near future for the hard work he had put into his father's business. If the business went to pot under his brother Patrick's immature, irresponsible direction (the outsider, Mickey, was great in the field but not a candidate for front-office management), then Tom Jr. would never get anything out of the business. If he did not quit, however, he might only be setting himself up for the same dilemma a year hence, when twice as much accumulated equity would be at stake.

Figure 7. Sustained conflict in the Flanagan family.

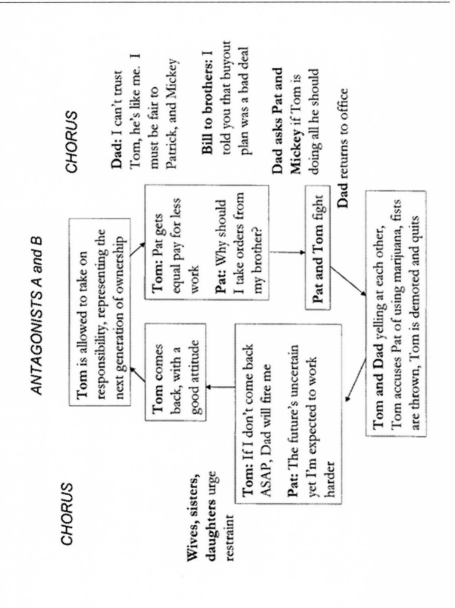

My sketch of their conflict, along the lines of Figure 7, led me to support Tom Jr.'s insistence on reopening the whole succession plan. I advised Tom Sr. privately that he needed to make a decision: Was it his purpose to maximize his financial return for retirement purposes, or to pass along a successful business to Mickey and one or more of his sons? If the company were to grow and prosper in their hands, he could not go on defining the problem as Tom Jr.'s "making up his mind whether he wants to be a company president or a street fighter." He would have to retain leadership long enough to break his sons out of that cycle. Showing him the sustained conflict cycle chart (always an effective visual aid), I said that I believed that Patrick was as much a troublemaker as Tom Jr. was, but that the real cause of the trouble was their inadequate preparation for his retirement. I tactfully pointed out his own role in perpetuating the problem—his demoting Tom Jr. to Patrick's level every time the brothers had a fight (which gave Patrick an incentive to pull his brother's trigger), instead of rewarding both sons for managerial development.

Unfortunately for the company, but perhaps fortunately for Tom Jr., his father continued to blame him for the battles between the two of them and between the brothers. As a psychotherapist, I could not help seeing Tom's unresolved anger, disappointment, and hurt at his son's misspent youth. I saw his resistance to acknowledging that Tom Jr.'s volatile temper was a carbon copy of his own, and I saw that Tom Jr. had reopened the wounds that his brother Bill had inflicted by rejecting their father's ownership transfer plan. I ended up keeping these insights largely to myself, however, for this family was not interested in them; the family members simply wanted to know whether the take-it-or-leave-it plan could work or not. I thought not.

Family conflicts sometimes echo patterns belonging to the family's cultural heritage, even generations after the migration to America. It is interesting to observe that Irish fathers usually did not decide until late in life which son would inherit the land (McGoldrick and Pearce, 1981). Today, Tom Flanagan Sr. is still running his business. The firm did buy back Tom Jr.'s stock. Patrick and Mickey now own a majority of the shares, but the future is less clear than it seemed three years ago.

Tom Jr. benefited from seeing the cycle he had been trapped in. He found a good hourly electrician's job with the large firm where his father had worked for thirty years. In less than a year, he was promoted to the front office. His brother Bill has a similar managerial position with a construction company. They have talked about starting a business together, when the time is right.

Consultant or Therapist?

The Flanagans required a consultant essentially to manage a necessary confrontation. Charting the cycle gave me a map through the conflict and a vivid picture with which to confront the parties. If Tom Sr. had allowed me to do so, I could have moved into a family counselor's role (or referred him to an appropriate professional) to help deal with the emotional issues between him and his sons. Still, it did not require a therapist to see that Tom Sr.'s succession plan was ill advised and unequitable. One need not be a mental health professional to make good use of analyzing sustained conflict cycles and shared fear.

In general, I do not believe that an expert on family systems should be a member of every professional team advising business owners on succession matters. Obviously, attorneys and accountants must always be involved, and each case will call for other organizational and financial consultants but not always for a therapist. When can these methods be used by anyone who is analyzing the organization? When is it better to bring an expert on family systems on the scene?

Often a nonpsychologist can trace a sustained conflict cycle on the basis of what the involved parties report. Any consultant can fill in the diagram and use the arrows (see Figure 3) for guidance on the parties' shared apprehensions and their healthy adjustments. If there are blanks in the cycle, "what if" questions can be used. Clients themselves, and their consultant's relationship with them, will make it clear if and when the issues call for a process person rather than a technical adviser.

An attorney or financial adviser can often ask "what if" questions, clarify consistencies and inconsistencies among different individuals' answers, and even suggest constructive actions. For example, "You ought to tell your son" is not an intervention that requires a therapy license. Where one should draw the line is at the point of offering to intervene in emotion-laden communications. "Can I help you say that to your son?" or "I'm surprised none of you expressed your grief and fear" would probably be inappropriate for an attorney to say, just as it would be inappropriate for me to give estate planning advice. When there is work to do on the other side of that line, the attorney or other professional should consider whether to bring a psychologist consultant into the case or simply refer the client to an appropriate treatment program or a private mental health professional. Before making either suggestion, it may be best to call the person or the program one has in mind for the client, discuss the problem anonymously, and get specific advice for making the referral responsibly, effectively, and tactfully in the particular situation.

Why do consultants do that less often than they should? For example, in the case of a family, one of whose members appears to have a drinking or drug problem, why are consultants shy about confronting the problem? But "why" is the wrong question. If we ask, "What would happen if...?" we may learn that many consultants fear offending their clients. Our next question should be whether what they gain by not offending their clients is really worth more, in the long run, than what they lose by not helping their clients.

There are cases in which one sees the sustained conflict cycle but cannot get to the root of the parties' shared fear, even when they have been interviewed privately. That is a situation in which one probably does need a co-consultant who is a family therapist. The terminology causes confusion here, because even when a family therapist is consulted, it does not necessarily mean that the family needs to engage in therapy. It means that the family needs a consultant who is trained and experienced in therapeutic counseling with many kinds of families in all kinds of distress, including but not limited to business-owning families.

It should be pointed out that not all clinical psychologists, not all clinical social workers, and only a small number of psychiatrists are formally trained to work with family systems. Conversely, designations like *family therapist, family counselor,* and *family systems specialist* may, unfortunately, be used by people with little or no clinical training. Other professional consultants and their clients should ask detailed questions about our certification and experience, just as we would probe a legal or financial consultant's experience and knowledge about closely held businesses before referring anyone to him or her.

Summary

Family business disputes are often examples of a type of conflict whose most significant features do not fit the prevailing dispute-resolution models. Members of a family (or, in fact, of any familylike group of co-workers) quite often are fighting about deeper issues than the ones they claim to be incensed about. Clear communication is at least as crucial within family systems as it is between any other disputing parties, but it is never true that family members need only understand one another's positions, common interests, and respective differences to work rationally together toward an optimal resolution. Often, unfortunately, their reasons for sustaining their conflict—reasons probably not even clear to themselves—are stronger than their ostensible desires to resolve it.

Fortunately, while disputes among people who have long-term relationships with one another add an extra dimension, by contrast with the average contract negotiation or tort litigation, such disputes have their own chronic, repeated dynamics, which an observer or interviewer can chart. The chart, once filled in, shows the typical course of conflict escalation in this group, including who does what to whom and what function the conflict serves. It also shows what the members normally do to keep the conflict within bounds, information that a consultant can use to strengthen the system's healthy resources.

My background in problem-centered family systems therapy has taught me to ask questions of the form "What would happen if...?" This is an unthreatening way to make constructive suggestions. It is also the least provocative way to explore any shared fears or assumptions that have kept family members laboring on the stationary bicycle of stultifying conflict. Although other consultants to family businesses will neither want nor be expected to operate as therapists, the analytical tool of the sustained conflict cycle, as well as the interviewing device of the "what if" question, can be incorporated into any skilled consultant's repertoire, without danger of the consultant's overstepping the boundaries of his or her own professional expertise.

References

Bateson, G. *Steps to an Ecology of Mind*. New York: Ballantine, 1972.

Blake, R.R., and Mouton, J.S. *Solving Costly Organizational Conflicts: Achieving Intergroup Trust, Cooperation, and Teamwork*. San Francisco: Jossey-Bass, 1984.

Coser, L. *The Functions of Social Conflict*. Glencoe, Ill.: Free Press, 1956.

Deutsch, M. *The Resolution of Conflict: Constructive and Destructive Processes*. New Haven, Conn.: Yale University Press, 1973.

Fisher, R., and Ury, W. *Getting to Yes: Negotiating Agreement Without Giving In*. Boston: Houghton Mifflin, 1981.

Kaye, K. Toward a Developmental Psychology of the Family. In L. L'Abate (ed.), *The Handbook of Family Psychology and Therapy*. Vol. 1. Homewood, Ill.: Dorsey Press, 1985.

Lewin, K. *Resolving Social Conflicts*. New York: Harper & Row, 1948.

McGoldrick, M., and Pearce, J. Family Therapy with Irish-Americans. *Family Process*, 1981, 20, 223-241.

Miller, E.J. and Rice, A.K. *Systems of Organization: The Control of Task and Sentient Boundaries.* New York: Barnes & Noble, 1970.

Pinsof, W. *Integrative Problem-Centered*
   Therapy: A Synthesis of Family, Individual, and Biological Therapies. New York: HarperCollins, 1995.

Putnam, L. Bargaining as Task and Process: Multiple Functions of Interaction Sequences. In R.L. Street, Jr. and J.N. Cappella (eds.), *Sequence and Pattern in Communicative Behavior.* London: Edward Arnold, 1985.

Simmel, G. *The Sociology of Georg Simmel.* Glencoe, Ill.: Free Press, 1950.

Ury, W.L., Brett, J.M., and Goldberg, S.B. *Getting Disputes Resolved: Designing Systems to Cut the Costs of Conflict.* San Francisco: Jossey-Bass, 1988.

Weber, M. *The Theory of Social and Economic Organization.* New York: Oxford University Press, 1947.

§

THE ADVISORS who work primarily or exclusively with family firms come from widely divergent professional disciplines. Through organizations like the Family Firm Institute, we learn from one another's perspectives. But we also grapple with fundamental differences, which affect how we see our responsibilities and what we consider ethical standards.

I discussed the problem of who our client is and how to serve multiple family members' contradictory and sometimes secret agendas, in FFI's newsletter in 1992. The same issues were still on my mind twelve years later when I wrote the article with Sara Hamilton on "Roles of Trust in Consulting to Financial Families."

§

Who's the Client?*

Afamily business consultant serves the whole system: nice idea, in principle, but what do we do about the fact that individual members' goals are sometimes incompatible?

Attorneys, who necessarily represent only one party in any potential conflict, tend to intensify differences. We non-attorneys sometimes accuse them of having a personal stake in win/lose outcomes. Representing an individual party is fundamentally at odds with family systems thinking.

On the other hand, the family therapist's approach, trying to facilitate the "client system's" win/win resolution of problems, requires us to understand each person's position and gain individual support for the group process. To that end, as well as to avoid surprises and to learn as much as possible about latent issues that may need to be brought out in the group, we typically conduct interviews privately with each individual or couple, encouraging them to speak candidly, in confidence.

"I won't tell Dad, but my first move as president would be to fire both my brothers. He feels sorry for them; I don't." (A youngest son who publicly subscribed to family loyalty.)

"Between you and me, I don't care if I never see another chrysanthemum as long as I live. But if my mother knew that, she'd give the nurseries to my sister or sell them at a ridiculously low price. So Jack and I have to pretend we want to move back here and be part of the business just as Mom wishes we would. Of course Sally's going to get the business, but it's going to cost her plenty! The best defense is a good offense." (An MBA who had moved out-of-state years ago and had no horticulture experience.)

The better we do our jobs, the more likely we are to learn in this manner that one or more members of our client system aren't negotiating in good faith.

---

*   Family Firm Institute *Newsletter*, Fall 1992. Reprinted with permission, all rights reserved.

To prevent that, some family therapists meet only with the whole system, or refuse in advance to keep any secrets. They emphasize that they aren't responsible for the problem or its solution—only for facilitating the process of discussion.

In my view, such therapists are playing a game with their clients more than they are serving them. It is not true that we consultants are mere facilitators. We are hired for our "expert" advice based on others' successes and failures. We are hired because we know something about which kinds of change are possible and which kinds are unlikely to occur. True, the clients must own the problem, make the decisions, and do the changing; but they certainly expect suggestions, and we earn our fees by basing those suggestions on the best information we can gather.

Better than avoiding secrets, I think, is making it clear to all that I will keep specific confidences but that my advice will definitely be influenced by them.

In the case of the sister who admitted (boasted, actually) that she was lying to her mother and sister, I said in the presence of all concerned that I had learned enough to convince me that the sisters and brothers-in-law would not be able to work together and that Mom should accept the disappointment. I went even further in private conversations with the company's accountant and Mom's estate attorney. Without quoting the out-of-state sister verbatim, I let those advisors know that I was sure her alleged interest in moving back was an insincere ploy. This verged on violating confidentiality and taking sides, yet to be "neutral" would be a grave disservice to Mom, who was both my client (as sole owner of the company) and the elderly victim, I felt, of emotional abuse.

In the case of the son who was planning his brothers' severance, I was able to persuade him to say so to his parents himself. My conduct in that case may seem less questionable; yet it turned out that this instance of honesty was not the best policy for achieving his selfish interests.

These cases aren't exceptional: they are typical. They raise therapeutic, ethical, and practical issues all at once. The consequences of mishandling them are impossible to overestimate. Yet, it is irresponsible and unhelpful to ignore them. In short, this is an area of consulting practice that warrants ongoing debate.

§

I'VE ALWAYS been intrigued by patterns that recur across families, especially when they transcend regions, cultures, wealth and other variables. One of the first such patterns I noticed in family firms was the situation I call "prisoners of the family business." The "kid brother syndrome" is a subcategory of that.

I continue to encounter "kid brother" cases, as well as other forms of imprisonment in the family business, and I'd make the same observations today as I did in this article written more than a dozen years ago. Unfortunately, I haven't found any better tools for helping them escape.

§

The Kid Brother*

Structural family dynamics that place one sibling in an outsider role can have powerful repercussions in the family business. This article draws on case examples to illustrate a pattern afflicting some youngest sons that may result from such a process. The author discusses approaches to preventing such a pattern.

"HE'S ALWAYS got an excuse, it's always somebody else's fault."

"The problem is, my parents spoiled him."

"He is the smartest one of the four of us; the most educated, and he has tremendous potential. There's nothing he couldn't do if he would only apply himself. But he ambles in an hour after we open, he's on the phone with his friends more than he is with customers, and often he's gone by mid-afternoon."

"He is never wrong."

"You know, he accuses me of being autocratic. He'll tell you I ignore his ideas. But the truth is I bend over backwards to try things his way, in hopes that he'll take responsibility. He doesn't want to be held accountable. What he wants is to complain."

Those quotations come from the author's notes taken during interviews with clients: five *different* clients. Although the five speakers could be describing the same person, each is complaining about his or her own youngest brother.

In these families and presumably many others, parents and adult children—like their key employees and professional advisers—use similar terms to describe problems with the youngest son. They regard him either as inadequate or as potentially able but unmotivated, lazy, incompetent, difficult to work with,

* *Family Business Review*, 1992, Vol. V, pp. 237-256. Reprinted with permission from the Family Firm Institute, Inc. All rights reserved. The author thanks Edwin Crego, Peter Williams, and Donald Crampton for their comments on an early draft of this article.

unreliable, or irresponsible. Yet he not only receives financial support from the family, he does so through continued employment by the business despite their constant complaints about his poor performance.

The kid brother syndrome

For purposes of this discussion, the "kid brother" could be anyone in a family business with at least one other sibling. He isn't necessarily younger; but we shall use the word *kid* because it often happens that the youngest brother takes this role.

There may be some sisters who fit this description; but as the author has encountered no female exemplars of the syndrome, the word *brother* and male pronouns will be used.

The word *kid* has another connotation, evoking the scapegoat referred to in the Old Testament (Leviticus 16). In my experience, the typical kid brother is neither a wholly innocent scapegoat nor a justly accused scoundrel. Perhaps he has been cast in a role; but then he plays that role all too well. He may repeatedly confirm some or all of his family's negative expectations; yet those expectations can be traced back to prior experience with him. The kid brother syndrome is an attribute of the family business system as a whole, defined by the conjunction of its members' negative perceptions and complaints about him with their concerted efforts to retain him in the business.

Although they appear in a broad spectrum of family businesses, four specific features may be observed with surprising regularity. First, the family member bearing these symptoms is, in many cases, so much younger as to have been raised in a more affluent family with a somewhat different value system than the ones his older siblings knew. In six of the ten cases listed in Table 1, the kid brother was eight to 22 years younger than his oldest brother or sister and five to 15 years younger than the "star" brother in the family business. In all six of those cases, parents and siblings suggested that wealth may have been a significant factor in "his problem." More than one referred to it as a "generation gap" within the sibship. Broader-based research would be needed to determine whether the size of the age gap is actually an important component of this syndrome.

Second, in those cases where I have had the opportunity to observe the kid brother's interaction with others or to interview him directly, I have quickly come to share the family's exasperation with his unfortunate tendency toward defensiveness and making excuses. The kid brother has a ready list of counteraccusations or other justifications for his deficient performance. Sometimes he even suggests that others are using him as a scapegoat. As indicated in Table 1, at least eight of these kid brothers went far beyond the normal defensiveness we all display at times—to the point where it prevented them from engaging in self-examination and from acknowledging their contributions to any problem.

Third, whether or not their parents agree with the complaints by harder-working children about the kid brother (indeed, the parents may be deceased or no longer active in the business), the family feels an obligation to carry him along. They feel he is entitled, as his birthright, to at least a nominal position in senior management. They may even pretend that he is a candidate for leadership some day. Privately, however, all agree they would never entrust significant responsibility to him.

Fourth, the kid brother is trapped, before long, in the business. He and his family—and the consultant, too—see his alternative career prospects diminishing with every month that passes. This is not simply a tragic consequence of the kid brother's having fallen into the role of family frustrator. The whole family's fear that he wouldn't succeed anywhere else may cause them to perpetuate both his failure and his infuriating defensiveness.

The ten cases listed in Table 1 represent all those among the author's family business clients within a three-year period in which a sibling employed in the business constantly disappointed and frustrated the rest of the family.[1] As the ten cases span a range of European-American heritages (Irish, Greek, Norwegian, Croatian, English, Dutch, German, and Jewish) and the siblings span five decades of American youth, this syndrome appears to be culturally widespread. Nor is it confined to any particular type of business; these cases represent real estate development, food services, importing/wholesaling, bottling, cattle ranching, construction, and four manufacturing firms.

Eight of the ten families described the company founders—the fathers—as men who didn't know how to express love or approval to their children except through material gifts. However, that might be a failing of entrepreneurial fathers in general. A larger sample would be needed to identify it as a causal factor in the kid brother syndrome.

Brief descriptions will serve to illustrate the great range of differences among these families. One case, J, will then be discussed in detail.

Cases A and B have been described previously in this journal (Kaye, 1991). One involved a father whose rivalry with his hardworking older son caused him

---

1. The fact that these were one third of his family business clients over the period surveyed is unrepresentative; the nature of the author's practice would attract this type of referral from other professionals.

to deny the youngest son's marijuana problem. The other involved twin sons whose constant arguing enabled their family to avoid facing the father's terminal illness.

Table 1. Ten "Kid Brothers"

	Foun-der age	Spouse age	Ages of children	Kid brother: alcohol or drug abuse?	defensive, many excuses?
A	_61_	_59_	_38_* **36*** _35_ 33 31 **26**~ _19_	Yes	Yes
B	_57_	_58_	35* 33~ **31 31**~	No	Yes
C	†	_92_	_70_ **63*** **48**~	No	Yes
D	_63_	_70_	_40_ **37 34*** **29**~	No	Yes
E	_60_	†	36 **35*** **32**~ _31_ 29~	Yes	Yes
F	_67_	_68_	**42*** **40** † _34_ **32**~	Yes	?
G	75	_70_	50 48 **47*** **43**~	Yes	Yes
H	_83_	_74_	**50**~ **47*** _42_~	No	?
I	_63_	_64_	44 42 **40*** _38_ **34**~	Yes	Yes
J	78	_72_	48 **46*** **40**~	No	Yes

Boldfaced ages are men ; *italicized ages are women.*
<u>Underlined</u> are the ages of those members who worked in the business at the time the author was consulted.
† deceased family member
* a family "star"
~ a family disappointment or embarrassment (all but one are youngest males)

Company C's founder had died fifteen years earlier, when his sons were forty-eight and thirty-three years old. The elder had run the company ever since (with his sister as office manager), and the youngest now felt that it was his turn. He was a knowledgeable, hard-working engineer; but his sixty-three-year-old brother (two of whose sons now managed sales and marketing for the company) had no confidence in the younger brother's decision-making ability.

Case D was an entrepreneur one of whose sons had become a workaholic like himself. His other three children fell far short of his expectations—especially the youngest son, who consistently came to work late, sneaked away early and by his own admission "hid out" most of the time in between.

In case E, two sisters and their husbands were the leaders of both family and business. The oldest son might have been the leading candidate for president but for the family's concern about his alcohol abuse. He was made to look good by comparison with the defiance and inflated sense of entitlement of his two younger brothers, one in the business and the other unemployed but an equal owner.

In case F, both the forty-and thirty-two-year-old brothers had a history of drug problems; the forty-year-old was in recovery. Their older brother was clinically depressed, feeling the whole burden of responsibility on him to fulfill his father's high expectations.

Client G had purchased most of the family farm from his father, but he now employed his youngest brother who was an alcoholic and extremely unreliable.

Case H was an exception in that the nonperformer in the business was older than the "star" brother. Childhood epilepsy had held him back, which may have shifted firstborn-like pressures onto the next brother. The family also patronized their "baby" sister, whose ex-husband had been a kind of kid brother-in-law. Although an acclaimed nonperformer, he was not fired until more than a year after they were divorced.

Case I possessed all four characteristics mentioned above: the age gap, the master of excuses, the family's simultaneous complaints and protection ("codependency"), and the fact that the youngest brother appeared to be a prisoner of his family's business. Despite great differences in cultural heritage and education between this case and case D, their complaints and excuses were almost identical.

The configurations in Table 1 strongly indicate that factors other than chance make this a kid *brother* syndrome. The mathematical probability that eleven out of the twelve siblings displaying these disappointing qualities would happen to be sons by chance, in a sample of twenty-four sons and eighteen daughters, is less than three chances in 1,000. The fact that the villain or cad in these cases is so often the youngest son proves that something more is at work here than the magnification of inborn deficits in competence, reliability, or drive. The probability of their appearing by chance in the birth positions shown in Table 1 (or later) is less than one in 100. (Any congenital traits would almost certainly be distributed randomly among the siblings; traits linked to the male chromosome would be distributed randomly among the brothers.)

"Ego Builders"[2]

Case J lends itself to detailed discussion because it possessed all four "typical" characteristics of the syndrome and presented several critical consulting issues. Ezra Berger looked like a dedicated member of the family business. He put in exemplary hours, dressed sharp, was never late for a meeting, and he complained that his forty-six-year-old brother, Dan, president of Ego Builders, didn't give him enough to do. Dan and their father, still principal owner of the company, agreed that Ezra had not performed satisfactorily in any area of the business. As Vice President for Special Projects, forty-year-old Ezra occupied a solitary limb of his own on the organization tree. None of the 150 employees reported to him. Ezra supposedly reported to Dan, but he rarely had anything to report. Managers complained that Ezra's presence in their meetings was more obstructive than helpful, and his brother Dan felt the same way. Yet Jack and Fran tended to side with their younger son. Without claiming that he was competent to hold a position of responsibility, they begged Dan to find some way of making Ezra feel he was contributing. The two sons drew equal salaries.

Jack Berger had founded Ego Builders with his brother Barney in 1947. Sons of an immigrant carpenter who had never learned English, they had entered the building trades in their early teens. Jack, the elder brother by ten years, had worked his way through college and later went back for an engineering degree. Barney, less educated and less ambitious, was a good salesman for the company. Jack's side of the family said that Barney never pulled his weight, but his sudden death in 1989 left his widow and daughters with 49 per cent of the Ego stock. One of Barney's sons-in-law, Bert, was vice president for sales; and Barney's widow, Selma, was nominally a member of the board (Figure 1).

Just over half of the shares were owned by a holding company controlled by Jack and his wife Fran. Each of their three children owned one tenth the Franjac company's shares, making them five per cent owners of Ego Builders. However, the shares paid no dividend, Franjac had to vote as a single unit on the Ego board, and there was no provision for either Ego or Franjac to buy back any individual's shares.

Jack had retired as president of Ego Builders in 1987, after surviving his third heart attack. Jack and Fran hired me in 1990 because they were at their wits' end over the constant battle between their sons Dan and Ezra.

---

2.   All individuals' names and the nature of their business, but no significant details, have been altered.

Figure 1. The Berger Family. <u>Underlined</u> members worked in the business.

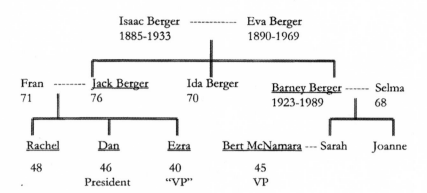

Jack and Fran tried to be evenhanded in apportioning blame to the two sons. They told me that "everyone complains about Dan's temper." He yelled at the office staff, including his brother Ezra; and he yelled at his parents, who believed Ezra's charge that Dan refused to give him anything to do. At the same time, their father was the first to say that Ezra had contributed nothing of value in the eighteen years he had worked for Ego Builders. Jack himself had pulled Ezra out of sales because he kept offending customers; and it was Jack who had adopted the unfortunate recommendation of a respected consulting firm, putting Ezra in the Special Projects cul de sac and Dan in the role of president.

It infuriated Dan to have to answer his father's questions and endure Jack's "broken-record" commentary about the profit margins he used to maintain, compared with Dan's current narrower margin; or to be reminded about the time Jack found the loading dock door open, an invitation to thieves and peddlers, and Dan told him "It's not the president's job to go out back and investigate who left the door open." (Dan was working hard to develop accountability at all levels, in direct contrast to his father's "nose in everything" style.)

Dan began to do something about his temper soon after the consultation began. He met with me individually on a weekly basis for a blend of personal therapy and management counseling; and he was sincerely interested in changing. Ezra, however, was sincerely interested in blaming Dan. The meetings I held with both of them together went like this:

> EZRA: "You never give me any projects to do."
> DAN: "You're supposed to be taking initiative and proposing projects."

EZRA: "You'd shoot down anything I would suggest."
DAN: "Try me."
EZRA: "No, I'm not going to set myself up for your criticism."

On one subject the two men agreed; it even rekindled a bond between them, as well as with their sister, whenever it was mentioned. This subject was their experience with their father throughout their lives. Having hurled accusations at one another a moment before, it was surprising how quickly they would unite when I raised questions about their early years or their business tutelage under their father and uncle. Jack Berger's negativism had left open wounds in his children. He had apparently never tempered his criticisms with praise or even approval. They told me that one of his typical "jokes" had been, "When you impress me, then I'll compliment you." When I asked him about that, Jack explained that his own father had never complimented him, either.

It was clear that Dan had become the target of the anger, hurt, defensiveness, and mistrust his sister and brother—and he himself—had long felt toward their father. As older brother, educational achiever, and tireless worker in the business, the transfer of their resentment from father to Dan was understandable—particularly as he hadn't learned to treat people any better than his father did. But was it equally inevitable that his younger brother should assume the role of a do-nothing with an unwarranted sense of entitlement?

The Inside Outsider

Some hints are to be found in psychoanalytic theories. Although Sigmund Freud overemphasized the triangle of father-mother-child, even his early followers (for example, Adler, 1956[3]) noticed the drama of sibling bonding, competition, and cooperation. A family-systems perspective is compatible with analyses of individual personality development that consider the meaning each member derives from family membership, from his or her own role in the family, and from relations with the others. A school of psychoanalytic thought called *object relations theory* particularly invites such family-systems considerations.

One object relations concept that may be familiar to the reader is the *transitional object* (Winnicott, 1965); for example, the blanket or teddy bear a young child wants to carry from bed to day-care center to grandmother's house. Security blankets allow young children to "internalize," or carry within their developing

---

3.   Schachter's (1959) and Toman's (1976) theories about the effects of sibling position on personality can be traced back to Adler's work in the 1920s.

selves, the experience of parental nurturing even as they spend more and more time away from the actual parents. Raising them to be separate, autonomous, confident adults involves maintaining all the love and encouragement they need while exposing them to just enough insecurity and disappointments that they can cope with and thus learn to internalize their own mastery in place of dependency.

The family-owned business is the ultimate transitional object, easing the harsh transition between the safety of home and the cold, cruel world. There is nothing wrong with that, for adults who acquired at least a normal degree of mastery and security in the early years of life. However, if a child's early years failed to provide mastery and security—whether through too little nurturing or too much—then he may still be seeking to meet those needs in adulthood. Unfortunately, the more he needs a security blanket the less well his family business can provide it, for at least two reasons. One is that even under the best conditions, the business cannot serve as a vehicle through which to separate from his family. They are right there. The other reason is that whatever dysfunctional patterns made the child's emotional life difficult may still be operative among the family members in the business. Indeed, he may still be expected to play the role they scripted for him in early childhood.

Another pertinent metaphor for the family business is a totem pole. The business serves as a massive icon for ritually worshipping one's progenitors as well as controlling one's successors. (In fact, Jack Berger frequently pointed to his father's toolbox in a showcase in Ego's office, when exhorting his sons to keep working together as he and his brother had.) In a family where children try to follow in their father's footsteps, each successive son is more likely to experience that alliance between his father and older brother(s) as unfairly punishing and denying, rather than guiding and nurturing. Totem poles usually combine both varieties of ancestor/spirit, the threatening one and the nurturing one. (They reflect a primal conflict that is inherent in the way human beings socialize their children: bonding with them, yet pushing them away.) The threatening aspect of that alliance among his elders is likely to overwhelm the nurturing aspect, as his siblings view him more as a contender or challenger than as a welcome peer. The later he comes in the birth order, the more he is compared with the siblings rather than being treated as a unique person on his own course of development. When he compares favorably or is favored by their father, there is an implied threat like the one perceived by Joseph's brothers in the Bible. Yet if he compares unfavorably, that provides the justification to reject or revile him.

In short, he is the family outsider whether the object of parental favor or not. As such, it is understandable that he might grow up defensive and irresponsible, blaming others, and "acting out" his entitlement to the family's goods.

From a family-systems perspective, an Ezra Berger might be protecting his older brother's status. It commonly happens in families that children diversify, as it were, to fill different personality niches (Bank and Kahn, 1982). Their differences are reinforced, while their similarities may be outweighed by the need to claim separate turf. If one child is shy, his brother or sister may be outgoing; one becomes "our family scientist," the second "our sports star." Some such force might operate in families where an older brother or sister has pre-empted the role of "hard-working successor to Dad." If Ezra were to apply himself at Ego Builders, he might threaten the turf already claimed by Dan. (In fact, if he were to leave and become successful elsewhere, that too could challenge Dan's status in the family. It is not a tremendous exaggeration to compare the kid brother's imprisonment within the business to that of several dukes, earls, and princes who inhabited the Tower of London between the twelfth and seventeenth centuries.)

Family therapists frequently speak of the appointed incompetent or identified patient in a family, where the members find it easier to isolate one individual for treatment than to subject the whole system to scrutiny. It is not unusual to find the youngest child in that role, showing symptoms such as school failure, drug abuse, religious cults, or even psychosis—all regarded by such therapists as Haley (1980) as symptoms of the family's unwillingness to move on through the life cycle.

Some families simply need a dunce, a lout, a klutz, a full-fledged jerk or even a black sheep to make other members feel or appear competent. All three of Jack Berger's children gave him and each other something to feel superior about. Rachel, as a woman born in 1940, had been expected to know nothing about business and had fulfilled that expectation. She also had married a man who had no more respect for her than her father had; when he left her, she was prepared to do nothing but live off alimony and the annual $10,000 distributions to her and each of her children from Jack and Fran.

Dan, the middle child, performed the role of the ill-mannered, ill-tempered arrogant "brain" of the family—earning far more condemnation of his personality than respect for his intellect and his two masters' degrees (in engineering and in business administration, both from prestigious universities). And Ezra, in precisely the opposite role, earned more condemnation for never getting anything done than appreciation for his personal qualities (for example, his stable marriage and determination to be the kind of supportive father Jack had never been.)

Whatever the cause, once a family member begins to reject responsibility or to complain about others' unfair expectations, he creates a vicious circle. The others, frustrated, see him negatively. Then, as a perpetual disappointment to them, he feels even less confident of his own ability to achieve anything. Simultaneously, others take on more responsibilities—partly to differentiate themselves from him. The gap widens. Less is expected of him. Yet, paradoxically, the less an individual feels respected or wanted by his father and by his family business, the more he may feel driven to blanket himself within it.

In short, the role of nonperformer in the family business is self-perpetuating, and everyone collaborates in keeping him in that role.

The tender trap

Then something even more tragic occurs: the sands of time slip away, eroding alternative opportunities. Family business dropouts must compete in the job market with men and women of equal ability and often better experience, whose salary expectations are more modest. Having enjoyed incomes two or four or eight times as much as their jobs were worth, with commensurate mortgages and school bills and vacations, they are trapped. They talk of starting or buying their own companies, but they have no capital. Their equity has no liquidity. Nor does their future inheritance have any current value.

They are being held hostage in the family business.

In some cases, including that of Ezra Berger, his family's belief in the kid brother's incompetence may lead them to create and maintain those financially entrapping conditions. Or they may fear a rupture in the family itself if he were to leave the business; perhaps that is why they do nothing to open the financial trap, at the same time they condemn his dependency on the family business.

Why attribute this to sinister forces? Why does a student of family systems regard the money trap as more than just an unfortunate, unintended circumstance? Because family members often work hard to resist the kid brother's moves toward independence.

For example, Fran had assented to the author's declaration, in our first meeting, that a successful outcome of our work would be either that her sons stopped fighting or that one of them left the business. However, when I told both sons frankly that if they weren't interested in changing themselves, they shouldn't expect anything to get better, and Ezra then told his parents he wanted to be extricated from his present and future ownership of the business, his parents balked. Fran referred to Jack's dream of having both sons carry on what he had started. When pressed, she acknowledged her real fear, which her older son Dan, too, had voiced privately. She said, "Ezra can't seem to live on a $160,000 salary. What happens if he takes his money out of Ego Builders or out of our estate now, invests it somewhere and fails? His wife's family doesn't have money. Who's going to bail them out?" Ezra's family expected to have to support him all his life. They could neither imagine him succeeding on his own nor imagine holding him accountable for his own failures.

Ounces of prevention

If ever there were a problem for which an ounce of prevention were worth a pound of cure, the kid brother problem must be it. If a family can see or a far-seeing adviser can tell them, when their children are just beginning to work for the business (or earlier), that they are at risk of developing the kid brother syndrome, professional advisers and successful business families agree that they should apply at least one kind of preventive medicine at once: establish clear, constructive expectations and performance evaluations. This author would add three other principles: raise responsible children in the first place, build teamwork into the family culture, and establish options for young adults to use family resources toward alternative careers if they and the family business turn out to be ill-matched.

Establish constructive expectations. Talking about expectations from the first day a son or daughter comes to work is the best way to avoid the painful confrontation of failures to meet expectations. The Berger case provides, I think, a poignant illustration of the need for job descriptions, policies, and performance reviews for every employee in the business, especially the owner's children. The goals of applying these policies to each son or daughter might include the following:

1. Children should be given the greatest likelihood of succeeding and growing through a career in this business. However, not all will do so. In case they don't:

2. The policies should be designed so as to teach truths about the real world—learned from failure, disappointment, and frustration—that enable a young man or woman to conclude "I'm not going to be happy with a career in this business" and to get out while the getting is good. (Experience in the family business may be as valuable a gift for those who move from it as for those who stay.) Some may even come back later, with maturity and experience.

3. Most important, it seems to me, is that the policies should give each son and daughter little or no chance to fail and stay. This is crucial, because the kid brother who fails and yet stays in his family's business soon looks like a loser to other potential employers as well as to himself.

The need for job descriptions and performance reviews has been so frequently and thoroughly discussed in the family business literature that nothing more need be said here. All ten cases listed in Table 1 were tragic examples of the disasters that result from failure to establish clear expectations and accountability.

Raise responsible children. This point may appear obvious. I mention it only because most discussions of preparing children to succeed in the family business begin with their entry into the business instead of with their entry into society. Yet their value systems may already be set by their early twenties: if not set in cement, then at least poured and drying. Problems having to do with accountability, teamwork, and work ethic owe their origin primarily to early experiences in school and the family—including the parents' responses to a child's behavior and to external events in the child's life. (There are haves and have-nots in our society with respect to values and self-esteem, irrespective of economic advantages.) As challenging and trying as parenthood can be, it is still easier to build values and expectations into children from infancy through adolescence than it is to reprogram them as adults.

Cultivate a team of differentiated siblings. Starting when their children are very young, parents also need to promote a family culture that balances between independence and loyalty among brothers and sisters. Differentiating the children from each other and from the parents doesn't necessarily entail rivalry or isolation (Cicirelli, 1985). The key is to foster such respect for their different qualities and interests that there is plenty of self-esteem to go around; no family member has to seek it at the expense of another. And when they come together, whether for business or pleasure, it must be by choice, not by guilt.

Establish liquidity options. This final principle will be more controversial. This author's experience leads to the conclusion that every business owner needs to establish mechanisms for transferring wealth so that individuals not employed in the business can make use of some of the family's accrued capital in other ventures, if necessary, during their parents' lifetimes. It might be worth stressing the term financial planning, as opposed to estate (that is, bequest) planning.

Those mechanisms themselves are outside the author's field of expertise. I hope this article stimulates contemplation and discourse among legal and financial advisers who serve family firms. Let me just make two general points.

First, we have a tradition of deferring inheritance to the end of the parents' life rather than to an appropriate time in the child's life. That makes no sense, from the point of view of human development, if parents possess more than enough wealth to live out their lives comfortably in any eventuality. If our tax laws discourage the dispersal of wealth among heirs who are old enough to manage it while young enough to put it to entrepreneurial use, then as one of Charles Dickens's characters said, "The law is an ass."

Emphasis upon tax considerations can have dreadful results, as has frequently been noted. For example, trusts that skip a generation may avoid some estate taxes but force the entrepreneur's children to stay in the family business whether it is a good place for them or not. Their salaries are their only liquid inheritance. For those who don't choose to go into the business in the first place, as Rachel Berger told me, "I was born a rich man's daughter and I guess I'll die a rich man's mother, without ever having had a dime of my own."

Second, the appropriate mechanisms will almost surely be different in every case depending upon, among other variables, the ages and needs of individuals in both generations, the nature (not just the size) of the family's assets, and fundamental value questions. The value questions include the following: some parents want their wealth to create unrestricted opportunities for their children and grandchildren; some, on the contrary, hope their wealth will channel descendants' activities in certain directions; still others only wish to create a modestly comfortable lifestyle while requiring their descendants to succeed or fail independently, as the wealth passes to charitable or cultural institutions. (None of these cases logically requires keeping the offspring waiting until the parents die.)

The human sciences have hardly touched the field of passing resources to children and grandchildren along with at least some of their parents' values, commitments, and dreams—without trapping them in business relationships with one another, in unsatisfying or unproductive careers, and in bondage to property. The kid brother syndrome is not a chapter in the handbook of personality types. It is a chapter in the age-old saga of family money and values.

Pounds of treatment

In this author's opinion, all business owners need to apply the first and last principles (establishing constructive expectations as well as alternative liquidity options) when bringing sons and daughters into their firms. However, a consultant advocating those principles will be too late to help many clients. They come in anguish and frustration, precisely because they did not receive or did not follow that advice ten or twenty years ago—or didn't instill responsibility and self-esteem thirty or forty years ago.

Notwithstanding our incomplete understanding of the causes of the kid brother syndrome, we can suggest two paramount principles for advisers who work with these families.

One principle is that the family members—parents, siblings, and spouses—need to confront their situation realistically. They need to talk frankly, at length, about a topic that may have been either taboo or mentioned only in angry outbursts and then dismissed: the fact that the business relationship with this family member is not working. The second principle is that advisers need to help the family explore alternatives for the kid brother outside the business.

The author's engagement with Ego Builders involved both those approaches.

Talking about the unthinkable. Has the process of creating a "kid brother" gone too far to be reversed? Often the crisis in the family business offers potential for a breakthrough and great personal growth—as was the case with several of the clients in Table 1. In other cases, however, including that of Ego Builders, it may be dangerous, destructive, or futile to urge accountability and performance criteria just because they should have been implemented years earlier.

Confronting the situation realistically means to stop pretending that bandages might be sufficient for a patient who is hemorrhaging. Does the kid brother want to change? Are others willing to change their own habitual behaviors that feed into his? If not, it would be a disservice to refer him to a seminar at the Wharton School or to propose a long course of therapy (individual or family). For example, if he has developed an alcohol, drug, or gambling addiction, nothing else can be addressed constructively. The addiction must be treated first, which will never happen until the individual knows he is at the end of his rope, which in turn can't happen so long as his family members go on denying the problem, covering for him, and playing out more rope.

Nor are the addictive disorders the worst scenarios, from the point of view of prospects for change. If the kid brother's behavior is what clinicians call *character-ological*, he has learned to defend so well against criticism that he may be incapable of acknowledging any part in the problem, ever—let alone changing.

More often, fortunately, the kid brother's behavior is determined by patterns of interaction in the family. Those patterns can change when members realize the parts they have all been playing, and when someone has the courage to be the first to deviate from the script.

In a meeting with Dan and Ezra Berger, I drew a matrix on the chartboard and asked the two brothers to fill in the cells (Figure 2). Dan was able to suggest improvements for himself as well as his younger brother. Ezra could not come up with anything for the lower right-hand cell of the chart. He said, "Do you want me to give lip service to something—which is all he's doing? To be honest, I don't think there's anything I should change unless I see a whole lot of change in him first." I asked how he felt about the two suggestions his brother had made in the upper right-hand cell. "The first one is a set-up," he said, "and the second one is the same old bullshit I've heard before. What's funny to one person may not be funny to another person—but I am who I am, you know?"

So long as he took that position, I told Ezra, there was nothing I could do to improve his relationship with his brother or to improve his position in the family business.

For a clinical diagnosis, one would need evidence that Ezra viewed all his relationships that way. That did not appear to be the case. He didn't blame his mistakes and lack of accomplishment on other people generally; only on his father and brother. He had good friends, was happily married, and was regarded as a good parent to his young children. Therefore I believed his hopelessness might be restricted to just the situation he was in at Ego Builders. The prognosis for him elsewhere might be good—if we could talk about his leaving the business without that being defined as a defeat, a rejection, and an admission of failure. Thus the consultant's role was to reframe the idea of Ezra leaving the business as a constructive possibility rather than the ultimate failure.

Figure 2. Chart from Session with Dan and Ezra

	Dan should change	Ezra should change
In Dan's opinion	Stop yelling at people Be more approving of Ezra	Take more initiative Don't make insulting "jokes" to customers and employees
In Ezra's opinion	Stop yelling at people Tell me what I've done right Make me production manager	

Exploring and expanding options. The second principle is that of exploring and expanding the family's options. If the kid brother is caught in a trap, pry it open.

Ezra was not the only member of the Berger family who was trapped. So were his brother Dan, the company president, and their sister Rachel. Dan felt trapped in that he had devoted his entire working career of twenty-five years to Ego Builders. If he were to leave now, he said, he could probably find a job or buy another business—but what if he were to stay another five or ten years and have his mother then make good on her threat to sell the company because of Ezra's aggravation?

Rachel's situation was worse. She did not have Dan's financial security—a bachelor, he had been saving about half his salary for years—and she also felt much less self-confident than he. But they shared the view that Ezra had no more right to cash out his share of Ego than they did. Dan said, "If the severance package is good, I'll quit and let him be president!"

When I raised the issue of their estate plan with Jack and Fran, Fran told me, "We trust our children completely. We know that they will make the right decisions and be fair to one another when the time comes." The problem was, I pointed out, the time she was talking about wouldn't come for many years. Her husband's health was poor, but hers was excellent, and she was only seventy-two. Her mother was ninety-seven.

I said, "You don't trust your children at all. You've made their decision for them. The way things are arranged right now, they cannot get out of Ego Builders while they're still young enough to do something with their supposed wealth." I persisted in such arguments over a period of several weeks, until Jack and Fran escaped to Scottsdale for the winter.

Meanwhile, I was encouraging Ezra to study his options. How trapped was he, really? I encouraged him to see a career counselor, and he began to look seriously at small manufacturing companies that were for sale. There was a part of Ezra that did not feel helpless or incompetent. He voiced some excitement about the idea of buying a business of his own. January of 1991 was a risky time to be thinking about venturing out into the business world apart from his family, but on the other hand it was also a time for picking up bargains.

The author and his fellow therapists have much to learn from financial professionals about the options available to an Ezra Berger. In England, Ireland, and Europe, where wealth traditionally passed only to one son, the others often emigrated to the "colonies" or other lands of opportunity. Where is the frontier today in which they can seek their fortune?

When Ezra decided seriously to find another way to support his wife and children, he faced a serious problem. They currently lived on his salary of $156,000 plus benefits, a car, and other perquisites. He had no savings other than the equity in his house. Ezra counted on coming into what he presumptuously called "my inheritance" before his children reached college age. (Based on his parents' current estate plan, this was unrealistic; if his mother lived to be his grandmother's age, he would be sixty-five and his children would be in their thirties before they inherited anything.) In the near term, he felt he needed about $500,000 to tide him over and allow him to invest in another business of some kind. Ezra therefore proposed a severance plan amounting to payments of $100,000 for each of the next five years. Although this would represent a savings to Ego Builders (there would be no need to replace him on the payroll), Ezra downplayed that fact. He did not care for the implication that he currently represented a useless charge on the company. On the contrary, Ezra very much wanted an acknowledgment that he was entitled to this money: he, Dan, and their cousin-in-law Bert had taken substantial cuts in salary several years ago, when business was down. Formerly they had each earned about $240,000. Ezra's proposal was based on the difference between that "baseline" salary and what they had received in recent years, a difference he labeled as "cumulative paid-in capital." It was important to him that he was asking only for his justly deserved deferred compensation, which Bert and Dan would probably make up to themselves as soon as he was out of the picture. In fact, he cared less about the precise number of dollars than about getting his family's agreement that he had the money coming to him.

The only basis on which Jack and Fran were prepared to "pay Ezra to leave" was precisely the opposite of the rationale he wanted.[4] They feared that the five-year payout he was demanding from Ego would only enable Ezra to do nothing for five years and then appear on their doorstep. Both parents, as well as Rachel and Dan, all expressed such attitudes to me privately. Yet when Ezra told them he knew they had no faith in him, they denied it. They went on patronizing him as they had always done.

The family discussed Ezra's proposal in an all-day meeting shortly after the parents returned from their winter in Scottsdale. Since I was aware of many negative feelings that members of this family characteristically shared behind one another's backs (for example, Ezra had complained about Dan to Rachel and to

---

4.   Complications resulting from the fact that Jack's family represented only half the company's ownership are not germane to the topic of this article.

his parents far more bitterly than ever to Dan's face), I encouraged candor. The family obliged by saying a number of things (all nasty) that they had never said openly before. Rachel said she had been a second class citizen all her life; Ezra predicted that Dan would run the company into the ground; Dan countered that Ezra's demand "for Ego money to solve a personal problem" was an attempt to bankrupt the company; Fran told Ezra "at forty years old to start taking responsibility for your own life," and Jack accused both Ezra and Rachel of trying to inherit prematurely. Four or five times in the course of the meeting, Jack repeated his refrain: It was "a crying shame" the boys couldn't manage to work together. At the end of the day, Jack's were the only dry eyes in the room.

When it became clear that no one but Ezra's wife supported his proposal, Ezra exploded—and threatened to sue the company. It was the first time such words had been uttered, and obviously a low point in my work with this family. But it is a very important point for this essay: Family members do not take each other to court, as a rule, just to adjust financial inequities. They often do so out of a desire to right long-standing emotional injuries, and the son who has felt picked on or cheated of his parents' love and respect by their favoritism toward older siblings is a prime risk to take his rage to a litigation attorney—especially if he has not found another way to dissipate their fortune.

Fortunately, Ezra cooled down. Two days after the retreat he told me, "I am an adult and it is time I gave up hoping for approval or respect from my father. I have to leave this company not only because I think my brother is a lousy president, but also so I can start getting my self-esteem from people who will take me on my own merits." He confided that he had recently concluded a couple of years' psychotherapy, and I congratulated him on the soundness of his attitude. Ezra was not "characterologically" paranoid. He was, like most of us, capable of regressing to infantile functioning when in the bosom of his family.

Fran eventually convinced Jack that they should help Ezra leave the business by making substantial gifts to all three children from their personal assets. In concert with the company's accountant and Fran and Jack's personal attorney, who was reviewing their estate plan, I persuaded them also to agree on a buy-sell formula for all shares, presently owned as well as to be inherited. This was a terrible sticking point for Jack and Fran, who still hoped to keep Ezra and Rachel entangled in Dan's management of the business through their board membership.

The senior Bergers viewed employment in Jack's business as opportunity for their sons, full of tremendous potential. Other than the higher education they had paid for long ago, Ego Builders was the only kind of opportunity they would think of providing. They viewed their non-business assets—about $5 million—as a cushion for themselves and, with whatever the company stock might someday be worth, a superfluous windfall for their grandchildren. Had they viewed their wealth (rather than just the business) as a source of potential opportunities for any or all of their children, they could have created financial options that might have precluded both the sons' feud and the daughter's and youngest son's impatience for them to die.

Business first, family first—or every man for himself?

Every "kid brother" case plunges us immediately into the question whether their business is a business first and foremost, or an enterprise subordinate to the family's needs and desires. If it is the latter, does it exist to satisfy the separate needs and desires of every family member, or some shared vision of their joint needs?

These questions must be addressed both from the clients' perspective and from the consultant's. Let us consider the clients' view first. How do they perceive their family business? Does *they* mean all of them, or most of them? Might the source of the tension be that they do not all have the same understanding of what a family business is?

In the Berger family, that was not the problem. Dan and his father were every bit as "family first" as Rachel, Ezra, and Fran. Dan would have been perfectly willing to ignore Ezra's nonperformance—if he would only shut up.

In other cases, however, and particularly when consultants become involved and advocate professionalizing the business management, different assumptions among the members could well heighten the tension between performers and nonperformers. But it could also turn up the heat on the younger sibling, whether performing or not.

In any case, the kid brother syndrome also raises the question about who the consultant's client is. Le Van (1991) has described the problem for attorneys, whose profession is based on advocacy for individuals or corporate entities and whose ethics block them from representing people who may be in conflict with one another. But the family therapist may have just the opposite problem. We are predisposed to advocate for the family's interest as a whole—but who determines what that is? The consultant may wind up resorting to a kind of "greatest good for the greatest number" strategy, which can easily lead to casting one member out. Especially if that member already feels inclined to liquidate his birthright. The scapegoat in the Old Testament was not sacrificed, but banished—unprotesting—to the wilderness (Jeter, 1990).

This author has no firm answer to the question of who or what the client is. I am certain, however, that there are better criteria for judging a family business to be successful than finding a place in the business for every member who wants one. I will not accept that criterion of success even when an entire family avows it.

It is important to reassure families that in releasing a son or daughter from financial bondage, they are simply freeing all their members to live and grow. Once having done so, they may well find themselves in business together, happily and successfully, ten years hence. But the latter can only happen as a result of voluntary commitments to their responsibilities, by all members. And in order to make voluntary choices, we must have options.

It is disquieting when a case culminates in a decision to let go of a dream. The case of Ego Builders will remain disquieting until time reveals how things turn out for Ezra, Rachel, and Dan.

Conclusion

The evidence adduced in this article is no more than suggestive. Therefore I assert only that the kid brother syndrome warrants attention, research, and discussion by advisers to family firms.

Since the method used here was analysis of cases rather than any statistical survey, we can do no more than speculate about the prevalence of this syndrome, or about its causes. The author hopes that others who work with or study family businesses will be led to consider their own experience with similar cases. As we compare our observations, their recurring features as well as the historical factors related to them should eventually suggest better forms of treatment or prevention.

If others' experience proves consistent with this author's, then treatment should emphasize realistically confronting the untenable situation and exploring and expanding other options for family members who show little sign of contributing to the business. Better yet would be to encourage business owners, at the time their children first come into the business, to establish constructive expectations and create liquidity options that will not require waiting for either the parents' or the business's demise.

References

Adler, A. *The Individual Psychology of Alfred Adler*. New York: Basic Books, 1956.

Bank, S.P., and Kahn, M.D. *The Sibling Bond*. New York: Basic Books, 1982.

Cicirelli, V.G. Sibling Relationships Throughout the Life Cycle. In L. L'Abate (ed.), *The Handbook of Family Psychology and Therapy.* Vol. I. Homewood, IL: Dorsey Press, 1985.

Haley, J. *Leaving Home.* New York: McGraw-Hill, 1980.

Jeter, K. Kings and Scapegoats in Twentieth Century Families and Corporations. *Marriage and Family Review,* 1990, 15, 225-240.

Kaye, K. Penetrating the Cycle of Sustained Conflict. *Family Business Review,* 1991, 4 (1), 21-44.

Le Van, G. Lawyers, Families, and Feelings: Representing the Family Relationship. *Probate and Property,* 1991, 5(1), 19-22.

Schachter, S. *The Psychology of Affiliation.* Stanford, CA: Stanford University Press, 1959.

Toman, W. *Family Constellation.* New York: Springer, 1976.

Winnicott, D.W. *The Maturational Processes and the Facilitating Environment.* New York: International Universities Press, 1965.

§

FAMILY BUSINESS magazine writer Jayne Pearl posed the question at the right to a panel of consultants. Although it's not a topic on which I've written anywhere else, I continue to find it an intriguing aspect of the diverse clientele I serve.

As I recall, the other contributors on the topic saw various advantages in strong religious faith for a business family. Perhaps reflecting my own religious skepticism, I listed as many disadvantages as advantages for those families who are what today we'd call "faith based."

§

When Faith Comes First*

Whether born-again Christian, Orthodox Jew, Muslim, or Mormon, many families believe their businesses must be guided by religious principles. Do strongly held beliefs help or hamper them in the pursuit of profit?

As a psychologist, I try to learn what an individual's or a family's faith does for their development, mental health, and success in life. From that point of view, it has not been my experience that religion—either the particular faith or the strength of conviction—has a predictable effect on the quality of family business functioning.

Recently, I heard family business advisor Léon Danco say that a family lacking a strong shared faith in God cannot hope to succeed in passing its business to the next generation. That is nonsense. There are many families who frankly admit they don't believe in God, yet transmit strong moral values and humanist commitments to their children and often succeed better in both business and family matters than theistic families. There are also many who give lip service to faith but violate it with their deeds—sometimes with dire consequences for their family and sometimes with no discernible consequences at all. So God is neither a guarantee of success in this world, nor a necessity for it.

A waste management company I worked with was beset by competitors using kickbacks and bribes to obtain contracts. Such practices are out of the question for this family, because of their strong moral principles. So they have had to compete on service and cost. They have succeeded, though not wildly. Religion hasn't given them an edge. If anything, it has created a challenge. It has motivated the family members to define the way they do business and strengthened their identification with one another. That could be a definite advantage in team building.

On the other hand, consider the reason they hired me. Their shared faith emphasized loving each other and suppressing anger. They avoided expressing disagreement; they felt guilty about desire for power in the family, and they were uncomfortable talking about wealth.

---

*   by permission of the publisher from Spring 1995 *Family Business* magazine, www.familybusinessmagazine.com.

Another deeply religious client wasn't sure whether it was morally okay to seek wealth. He had a substantial net worth on paper but was having trouble paying for his kids' higher education because he didn't feel entitled to liquidate stock—though it was publicly traded. To sell shares he had inherited, he felt, would be seen as materialistic and constitute irresponsible stewardship of an enterprise his parents had created to honor God. Feeling trapped and frustrated, he periodically attacked his brother, the CEO, at Board meetings and in letters to other family members.

I have worked with more than one firm whose faith is what I call "Word-driven" not spirit-driven. In these companies, directors and key managers—family and non-family alike—refer to Scripture verses in their memos just by the number, such as "II Kings 23." The clear implication often is: "Get out your Bible, sister-in-law, you're not being Christian enough today." They seem to do this wrathfully, judgmentally, self-righteously. Envy is apparent, and I wouldn't be surprised if gluttony and lust were, too, in some of these families. All the deadly sins.

Whether or not the advantages of faith-first businesses outweigh the disadvantages depends on many other characteristics, including the parents' personalities, the level of education in the family, the children's talents and personalities, and so forth.

The advantages include a shared basis of morality and values and a frequent discussion of values. As a result, they can say "We know what we think and what's important to each of us." The work ethic is thus reinforced by Scripture or Talmud; Jesus's parable of the talents, which teaches the value of building a return on investment rather than letting capital lie idle, comes to mind. The family's faith becomes part of its history, its identity, its reason for continuing to function as a team versus the outside world. In addition, for some families, the church, the parish, the synagogue, the Mormon stake are communities that function, in part, as business networks.

Disadvantages that I've seen in faith-first families include a fear of individuation; intolerance for dissent or different attitudes and lifestyles; self-censorship (often it doesn't even occur to the members to express negative emotions or disagreement); authoritarian parenting, which can leave children unskilled in conflict resolution; sexism (evangelical Christians, Mormons, and orthodox Jews are similar in their traditional subordination of women); confusion between the parent's will (in both senses of the word, *wants* and *bequests*) and God's will; self-righteousness; and for at least some Christians, ambivalence about whether it is all right to seek wealth.

§

TWO PROBLEMS of "entitlement" come up frequently in our work: too much or too little. A false sense of entitlement to wealth without responsibility has led to many a dissipated fortune. On the other hand, an insufficient sense of entitlement to inherited wealth can make capable, productive heirs feel inadequate.

§

Terms of Entitlement*

Offspring should feel that they have real value to contribute to the family business—and not that a career is handed to them on a silver platter.

"THE TROUBLE with young people today," my entrepreneur friend Walter recently said, "is that they think the world owes them a living."

He wasn't talking about his own two sons or daughter, mind you, with silver spoons firmly clenched in mouths. He was referring to other members of their "slacker" generation—those that run the gamut from disadvantaged dropouts demanding the government guarantee them jobs or increased welfare benefits to recent college graduates bemoaning the shortage of $40,000-a-year, entry-level positions.

Having worked his way up from almost nothing into ownership of a prosperous family business, Walter thinks other people should expect to work hard, too, for success in life. The word *entitlement* irks him. But ironically, by unconditionally guaranteeing his own offspring good positions and salaries at his firm, he's essentially running an entitlement program right within his own home: a form of "career welfare" for his kids.

The question of who's entitled to what in our society is debated in every election, but it's also controversial within our own families. Is every son *entitled* to a job in the family business, by virtue of his genetic lineage, whether he's qualified or not? What about daughters? Sons-in-law? Grandchildren?

Is it a matter of getting there first—like a client of mine who told his sons they could each succeed him as president for five years apiece, in their order of seniority? Or are family members due only the right to *compete* for jobs on the basis of qualifications and effort, just like the rest of the world?

There's no correct or easy answer. The extent of entitlement in a family business is a matter for the owners/parents to decide. Their shared understanding about company policy may be anything from "We'll find a job for every member

---

* reprinted by permission from *Corporate Detroit*, March 1996.

who wants to work here" to "No family members need apply." Most companies' policy falls somewhere in between those two extremes.

> The young person with doubts about his own worth often hides them under a blanket of arrogant behavior.

For example, it isn't unusual today for business owners to agree that family members should have to prove themselves, using the same criteria that applies to outside candidates. In still other examples, special compensation packages may be granted to family members, but performance may still be the criterion for advancement.

In his eagerness to have his children join him in the family business, Walter was afraid to set any conditions they might not meet. Speaking as a psychologist, I think Walter always confused love with money when it came to his children, and I know that in their youth, he confused supportiveness with sheltering them from the natural consequences of their own irresponsibility. As a result, one of his sons consistently behaves like a feckless jerk today, always blaming others for his failings. Wallowing in self-pity, this son feels betrayed, conspired against, unappreciated by everyone—in the business and in the family.

Conditional employment policies could have prevented his son's malady from contaminating the family business, but the whole problem of his sense of entitlement should have been addressed years earlier. Some individuals feel entitled to the benefits of ownership in the family business; some don't. That expectation can—surprisingly often—be totally unrelated to their actual qualifications, work experience and efforts.

Perpetuating a sense of entitlement begins in childhood—and human development is complex enough that the young person with deep doubts about his own worth often hides them under a blanket of cocky, arrogant behavior, a seemingly brash surface of entitlement that is, in fact, a defense mechanism against his profound feelings of unworthiness.

In other words, Walter's son *acts* as if he's entitled, paradoxically, because inside he really *doesn't* feel capable or deserving. He feels a deep-seated craving for respect, but because his father always pampered him and bailed him out of every tough situation, he has absolutely no confidence that he could ever earn a good career position the hard way, through his own intrinsic merits and demonstrated efforts.

Parents who want their children to be capable of managing responsible positions in society need to start building self-esteem very early by allowing them work and problem-solving experiences of various kinds throughout the school years. We must make our children feel entitled to *access* the resources our families are fortunate enough to possess, but at the same time, our children must also feel that they are indeed worthy by their own merits and achievements. Though our offspring may also share an inheritance someday just because we love them, that portion of the family's resources that are business assets should be invested in them today based on *performance,* not coddling and empty promise.

§

MURRAY BOWEN was among the first family therapists, and one of his seminal papers discussed how dysfunctional a family-owned business can be for individual development. Of course, literary authors had been saying that for centuries. There are examples in Freud's cases, too.

I believe my contribution to the field of family business research and advising has been to keep repeating and emphasizing that working together isn't necessarily healthy. Furthermore, as the following article insists, "in many cases the family business is not the patient but an illness afflicting the family. These are cases in which keeping it going means keeping the family sick. These owners *use their business to retard the normal development of their children and themselves*. Their health as a family business cannot be 'restored' because it isn't healthy for them *to be* a family business."

§

When the Family Business is a Sickness*

When a shared business retards the life-cycle development of both genera-tions, it may not be possible for consultants to "restore" their system to health as a family business, because it is unhealthy for such families to be in business together at all. Fantasies of saving their family business, or "succeeding" in passing it to the next generation, are misguided at best. The author argues that when parents' ego development is inadequate, normal individuation makes them and their children so anxious that the business functions like an addiction. A primary role of the consultant is to recognize such cases, diag-nose them carefully, and intervene in ways that encourage the next genera-tion to explore a wider range of options.

FAMILY BUSINESS THERAPISTS and financial/legal advisors hope to add to one another's understanding and not contradict one another's recommendations. Yet we survey the territory with different eyes. The latter group focuses more on suc-cess in terms of earnings, shareholder equity growth, and wealth retention; the therapists (of whom I am one) look at success in terms of individual and family development.

Across all our professions, however, most of the rhetoric about family business assumes that the desire of a next generation to enter and eventually take over their parents' enterprise is a good thing. Their firms and their families are described as suffering from various internal and external sources of stress, which unfortunately often interfere with their "success."

The mantra of the family business industry is that "only about one third of family firms *survive* to the second generation; at least two thirds *fail* to make it

*   *Family Business Review*, 1996, Vol. IX, pp, 347-368. Reprinted with permission from the Family Firm Institute, Inc. All rights reserved. The author thanks his many colleagues who responded to early drafts of the paper.

that far, and five sixths *fail* to make it to the third generation." Note the value-laden assumptions we reinforce every time we use those words *succeed*, *survive*, and *fail*. No one has calculated how many of the "failures" were actually terrific success stories, creating liquidity that opened new paths of opportunity for the next generation; or, conversely, how many that "made it" through a transition trapped their successors in misery.

We therapists have bought into those assumptions no less than the business and legal consultants. We address ourselves to problems such as the perfectionist, controlling nature which makes empowering others so difficult for many entrepreneurs; the frustration felt by successors trying to establish their competence and credibility under the shadow of a strong parent; effects on marital, sibling, and in-law relationships when a subset of family members interact frequently and intensely; the confusion between entitlement as an owner (present or future) and expectations as a manager; etc. Note that each such problem is assumed to afflict a system that is intrinsically worth fixing and preserving. These are problems we try to resolve so as to enable our clients to "succeed" in keeping their business in the family, rather than "fail" to pass it on.

When serious problems arise, the family business is treated, for all practical purposes, as a patient. Accountants, attorneys, financial planners, therapists and business consultants come to the bedside like a team of doctors, attributing the patient's condition to a combination of unfortunate causes and working heroically to restore the patient's health. The prescribed treatment is to improve decision-making processes and long range commitments by all concerned parties, with the help of experts in succession planning. We, the experts (regardless of professional discipline) tend to assume that the patient—the family's continuity in their business—must be saved. Because a family business is intrinsically good for its owners, its employees, its customers, and its community, it must be made healthy enough to survive.

That rhetorical picture may be consistent with our clients' dreams, but it isn't always true. On the contrary, in many cases the family business is not the patient but an illness afflicting the family. These are cases in which keeping it going means keeping the family sick. These owners *use their business to retard the normal development of their children and themselves*. Their health as a family business cannot be "restored" because it isn't healthy for them *to be* a family business.

The first part of this article describes families who relate to their businesses in unhealthy ways, as if it were an addiction. Then I offer an explanation of this phenomenon in terms of developmental psychology and family systems theory, specifically arguing that parents whose own ego development is inadequate tend to create family-shared apprehensions about individual differentiation, and thus may be inclined to use a business (unconsciously, and tragically) as a growth-retarding drug. In the final section, I discuss consultation to such families.

Because such cases are far from rare, a primary role of the consultant is to be able to recognize them, diagnose the problem, and intervene to encourage exploring a wider range of options for the next generation. Otherwise, a family-owned business can enable a dysfunctional family to maintain its dysfunction for decades, over generations; resisting individuals' efforts to achieve healthier roles and relationships, denying and distorting chemical or process addictions (for example, gambling); perpetuating conflict, justifying exploitation and excusing incompetence. Foolish parents and spoiled children can use a family business to cover a multitude of sins, especially the sin of claiming helplessness and victimization in the face of what is really their own self-destructive behavior. And because, like an addictive drug, the family business creates a "high" with delusions of grandeur and power, it creates a market for services that exploit those delusions and thereby, unfortunately, feeds the addiction.

Of course, there are also many healthy families in business. The achievement of a successful enterprise, the fun of managing it together, and the opportunity to use wealth beneficially excite their members in common cause and personal fulfillment, across generations. They are neither addicted to nor stifled by their enterprises—but this article is not about those families.

Context

Three directions influenced me to look at the cases where family business is a sickness. One was a series of astonishing statements by experienced family business consultants, about the high incidence of substance abuse among their clients. For example, Fredda Herz Brown (1994) remarked that virtually all her clients had one or more substance abusing members. Leslie Dashew (1995) said she found, if not alcohol or drugs, then gambling or some other addiction in practically every case. And Tom Hubler (1995) pointed out that "a family business is the ultimate enabler" to all kinds of addictions and dependencies. Such comments made me understand why one of the pioneers in our field, David Bork (1986), courageously put alcoholism at center stage by using an alcoholic family as the case example for his book *Family Business, Risky Business*.

No one has yet gathered data on whether substance abuse is much more prevalent in family firms than in US society generally. Regardless, when a business family does have a substance abusing member, is the substance addiction a cause or a symptomatic result of family and business problems? In my experience, the business itself is usually that family's primary drug, and various other dependencies follow.

The second influence upon my thinking came from consultants who questioned the reasons some people enter a family business. For example, John Messervey writes:

> Many enter the business as a means to resolve family issues of power, control, conflict and intimacy. These may include father-son conflicts, unresolved sibling rivalry or marital issues, and several dozen other challenges plaguing the family. So, the family business becomes the arena for desperately expected change, for repeated patterns of behavior and for acting out unspoken family conflicts. (Messervey, 1996)

"Desperately expected change" naturally leads to angrily experienced disappointment. Bernie Liebowitz's early insight has described many of my clients very well:

> Throughout their association in the FOB, both father and offspring appear to have been in a silent conspiracy not to allow underlying conflict to emerge and be resolved, even though when they started, each had hoped there would be a resolution that would satisfy everyone. (Leibowitz, 1986)

Leibowitz observed that family businesses are most often formed by people trying to resolve a problem in their relationship with a particular relative, or to fix a dysfunction in their whole family. Tragically, it doesn't work. It only perpetuates the problem, and sometimes makes it worse.

The third influence was my background as a developmental psychologist, which led me to interpret this tragedy in families as a matter of inadequate *differentiation*, or *individuation*. Successful human development is a balancing act between family attachments and the formation of a self. Family attachment is a strong instinctive motive, yet it works against individuation.

The three lines of thinking that converge in this paper are inherently intertwined, because addiction can be best understood (in family systems) as a failure of differentiation. Over-identification with a business is an example of a process addiction. What begins as a desperately sought solution becomes an even bigger problem; the enterprise itself becomes the drug of choice, with the whole family addicted to keeping some members in business together at all costs.

Unlike some of my colleagues, I see quite a few families who are free of chemical dependencies, gambling problems or other addictions. I cannot even say that I see workaholism in every case. Although they wouldn't come to me if they didn't have conflict, many are "clean-living" dedicated entrepreneurs with strong core values and cohesive families—sometimes *too* cohesive. Sometimes I see an addiction-like over-identification with a business, both generations clinging to it as if they were chemically dependent on it, even as it tears them apart.

Later in this article, I return to the problem of too cohesive families, and the idea that people might be drawn into family business in hopes of solving interpersonal problems. I shall argue that when a family business does become a process addiction, it may be a symptom of parental over control and resistance to children's individuation. First, however, we need to summarize some features that process addictions share with chemical dependence in families.

Troubling similarities

Schaef and Fassel (1988) point out that addictive organizations have essentially the same symptoms as do individual addicts and their families. Table 1 is a synopsis for purposes of discussion here, of the kinds of behavior that have been widely observed in addicted individuals and their families. Alcoholism is the most researched dependency illness, and the characteristics in Table 1 will be familiar to anyone who has worked with alcoholic families. However, they also characterize other chemical addictions as well as non-chemical addictions such as anorexia nervosa, bulimia, or gambling.

It is left to the reader to judge whether some of these characteristics are true of family firms he or she has known.

Progressive dependency and tolerance are the defining characteristics of any addiction. People are addicted to a substance or to a process when they will not give it up even though it is ruining their lives. *Tolerance* means that they tolerate more of it than the average person would—not that it doesn't affect them. The word *progressive* refers to the fact that it takes increasing doses to give them the "buzz" or other result they seek. *Codependents* are people who enable an addict to maintain his or her addiction.

Dependency is a central issue in many family firms. Inability to leave is the surest sign that a business is an addiction rather than a healthily shared enterprise. Just as one is an alcoholic when drinking is no longer a pleasure but a necessity, one is addicted to the family business when, without joy or fulfillment, one persists in pain. The way out seems more terrifying than the dependency is crippling. I described some entrepreneurs' children as "prisoners of the family business" (Kaye, 1992), but in truth their parents, siblings, or spouses are equally trapped.

Table 1. Characteristics of Addiction

---

1. Progressive dependency and tolerance

2. Denial

3. Defensiveness, projection, judgmentalism, invalidation of others' perceptions or ideas, dualistic (black-white) thinking, self-centeredness, isolation, tunnel vision, forgetfulness

4. Perfectionism and obsessiveness

5. Dishonesty, secrets, ethical deterioration, spiritual bankruptcy

6. Grandiosity, seduction, manipulative disinformation

7. Chronic stress, chronic depression, crisis orientation, negativism, fear, frozen feelings, external referencing (no feelings or perceptions of one's own)

Denial is among the most human mechanisms of mental life—used by normal, healthy, optimistic people every day. In the addicted personality, it predominates over realistic judgment, not only protecting the illness but guaranteeing its progression. The force of denial leads to the confused thinking and illogic faced by anyone who tries to confront addicts rationally.

Whole families engage in denial, in many ways. Families of workaholics can deny their disease easily, because workaholism carries no shame in our society. But their disease progresses, and until the organization faces reality, the individual cannot begin to recover. Similarly, prisoners of a family business suffer from their relatives' and friends' denials about the problem.

The third cluster of symptoms in Table 1 (the set beginning with *defensiveness*) have to do with shutting out information that threatens the addiction. Addicts and any codependent family members or co-workers are as quick to blame, criticize, and judge others as they are to defend vigilantly (proactively) against criticism of themselves. Often, in a family business, it is the norm to attribute interpersonal problems to "personality conflicts," implying that nothing is fundamentally wrong with the system. Thus its members cannot benefit from conflicting views as opportunities to challenge themselves and promote continual adaptive growth (Kaye, 1994).

Self-centeredness, isolation, and *tunnel vision* are common in addicts as they tune out possible threats to their status quo and as their chosen drug subsumes their world. Similarly, many business founders and successors have a remarkably narrow world view. The constant pressures of competition in a market economy naturally incline them to see government and labor unions as their enemies, inheritance as the only legitimate entitlement, and wealth itself as proof of pre-destination. Those precepts may become entangled with their faith, or even (for some) function as religious principles. Good vs. evil: Business ownership and tax avoidance are considered family values, while social welfare and regulation imply moral decay. Market protectionism is a patriotic virtue, but the same patriots advocate free trade when it comes to offshore cheap labor.

When speeches and newsletters on family business pander to the successful entrepreneur's sense of moral superiority (for example, with rhetoric about the rapaciousness of the IRS), they do both his family and society a disservice.

The first three clusters of symptoms in Table 1 probably lead to the fourth and also the fifth cluster. *Perfectionism* and *obsessiveness* result from a felt shortage of love, respect, or money (a surrogate for love and respect). The young child thinks, "If only I were more perfect, my parents would be happy and would value me." The grown-up child thinks, "If I achieve perfection (in my weight, my work, my social status, the cleanliness of my home, or whatever), *then* I'll be worthy of love." Many adults who are not addicts themselves, but were children of alcoholics, suffer from perfectionism, excessive self-criticism, workaholism, and rigidity.

Again, there is a parallel with family business: Scarcity of their father's attention and approval leads some adult children of entrepreneurs to workaholism and perpetual dissatisfaction with themselves. This underlies many sibling conflicts in family firms. Too little of what they need from either or both of their parents in childhood creates siblings who, as adults, will be chronically distrustful and jealous of one another. ("You were always the favorite.") This may explain why even some extraordinarily wealthy adults squabble like children over matters involving relatively few dollars.

Many of the symptoms in Table 1 are related to the need to control. For example, adult children of alcoholics make poor team members, according to Schaef and Fassel, because they are poor listeners, have difficulty giving and receiving criticism, and have an excessive need to control. Carrying the baggage of painful childhood experience into business relationships, their anxiety around authority figures takes the form of resistance or defiance, often passive-aggressively. Similarly, we see passive-aggressive behavior in not a few children of bossy entrepreneurs.

Codependents, on the other hand, are sensitive listeners, compliant, eager to please. "Codependents would rather care for someone in a way that leads to that person's death," wrote Schaef and Fassel (1988), "than to take the risk of seeing and speaking the truth and possibly offending him or her." In some business families, the favored successor may be the member least likely to challenge dysfunctional norms.

The fifth cluster includes *dishonesty* and *ethical deterioration* as well as the addicts' *spiritual bankruptcy*, which has been discussed explicitly by Hubler (1995) among other family business consultants. Religious faith is not equivalent to spiritual strength. Quite the contrary: religion can be a process addiction in itself, especially if parents are dogmatic and authoritarian instead of supporting each child's individualized growth in spirit and character.

The illusion of control through *secrets* in some (not all) business families is also a characteristic of addicts and their families.

Both the perfectionist tendencies and the dishonest tendencies are probably involved in creating the sixth set of characteristics in the literature. *Grandiosity* is frequently a characteristic of addicts. As they live on the verge of greatness, the promise of spectacular achievement or fortune keeps them from seeing how they are wasting their lives. The promise of the future takes attention away from current problems, denies current feelings, and devalues the ordinary self. The loftier and more unattainable the promise, the more probable that the organization becomes a rigidly grandiose denial system:

> The very fact of having goals frequently can be enough to con employees into believing that everything is all right in the organization. The mission is like a household god. As long as it is in its shrine, the organization is protected, even if what it is doing has little to do with the stated mission. (Schaef and Fassel, 1988)

Shared grandiosity plays into the *seduction* noted by addiction counselors as well as by consultants to addictive organizations:

> Loyalty to the organization becomes a fix when individuals become preoccupied with maintaining the organization. When loyalty to the organization becomes a substitute for living one's own life, then the company has become the addictive substance of choice....The issue is not benefits per se, but the way the organization and individuals use them to stay central in the lives of workers and consequently to prevent people from moving on and doing what they need to do. (Schaef and Fassel, 1988)

Seduction often takes a form that might be termed *manipulative disinformation*. Members are trapped in the family business, for example, by assurances that they can leave any time. Relatives are led to believe they have been promised management roles or financial rewards, then later accused of misunderstanding.

Finally, all of the above combined with desperation and unrealistic expectations naturally lead to *chronic stress, depression*, etc. Codependents are at especially high risk for workaholism (which ranks among the most resistant of addictions to treatment) and consequently for ulcers, colitis, back pain, high blood pressure, eating disorders. *Frozen feelings* and *external referencing* mean not knowing how one feels except in terms of what others want or expect one to feel. One has no boundaries, no self, and consequently no true recognition of others as selves with distinct feelings, perceptions, and desires.

> Most of these people want to be doing something else. When we challenge them to explore other opportunities, they respond that they cannot afford it. We should not miss the real message here:...they cannot afford to take the risk of being fully alive. (Schaef and Fassel, 1988)

Schaef and Fassel were writing about workaholic employees of corporations, but could they not just as well be describing prisoners of family business?

Surely we can identify some, if not all the problematic behavior listed in Table 1, in many family business systems. It is even clearer how similar family firms in pain are to families in chemical dependency if we describe the *progressive* course of addiction to family business. The downward decline is traced in Table 2, ending in a hopeless abyss. I drew the "crucial" and "chronic" phases of this table (with only a few word changes) from a poster widely used by substance abuse counselors, called a Jellinek chart. They use this to help members of addictive families recognize how far their illness has progressed, and where they are headed if they keep ignoring the problem. Earlier, in what I call the "relief" phase, the business might be used much like social drinking as an escape, complete with "peer pressure." Note that the risk factors for family business addiction are identical to those for substance abuse. (We turn to the "phases of recovery" side of the Jellinek chart later in this paper.)

Individual Development in the Nonindividuated Family

So far, I have only pointed out *similarity* between addictive families and a significant number of business-owning families. If indeed they appear to share similar symptoms, is it possible that the same processes might account for such developmental disturbances, irrespective of the substance or institution of choice?

Table 2. Phases of Addiction to the Family Business

1. Risk factors	Inadequate self esteem
	Inadequate skills
	Inadequate permission to differentiate (be an individual)
2. Relief phase	"Peer pressure:" sibling and/or parent encouragement
	"Escape:" family firm is a way to avoid competing in the real world
	Tolerance → dependence
	Guilt → denial and excuses
3. Crucial phase	Remorse, failure of resolutions
	Grandiose, aggressive behavior
	Loss of other interests
	Money troubles, denial of responsibility, blaming
	Lifestyle, inflated to compensate for emptiness, traps family member as dependent upon the business
4. Chronic phase	Loss of tolerance (too late)
	Lengthy "intoxications": obsession with the business
	Physical and moral deterioration
	Self-loathing → hopelessness
5. "Hits bottom"	

The function of normal parenthood is to develop independently self-supporting offspring. In developmental psychology, we call the progress of children toward self-support *differentiation*, or *individuation* (interchangeable terms).

Healthy adult children are separate, distinct people—even as they enjoy numerous interdependent connections with one another and with the other generations of their extended families. The field of family-business therapy has now progressed to the point where we can draw a powerful conclusion: Contrary to the course of normal life cycle development, family-managed enterprises are often used to *resist* the differentiation and development of children who join the business, and sometimes even of children who don't.

I am saying that *individuation and the family business are at odds.* This conclusion runs directly counter to the family business literature, which assumes that because processes of individuation in healthy families minimize destructive conflict and increase the chances of good succession, helping members to individuate should be good medicine for the less healthy family firm. On the contrary, I am concerned about the way family business succession in a less healthy family can be the means of resisting differentiation—maladaptively. In those cases, members' individuation threatens rather than supports the family business system.

The literature, unfortunately, often equates success with succession. For purposes of our discussion, we will *not* assume that succession to the next generation means the family business has succeeded. On the contrary, succession sometimes occurs as a result of developmental failure in a family, and (conversely) a thoroughly successful outcome for a family business can sometimes involve a decision to dispose of it. We are interested in the relationship between individuation and family business success—not necessarily succession.

What is "individuation"? "Individuation" is a lifelong developmental process that begins in the first year of life, soon after an infant begins to feel attachments to specific people. The infant becomes aware that relationships with parents, siblings, and other caregivers are vital for a body's physical and emotional survival. This translates into the importance of being needed and valued by those caregivers, which in turn leads to the question, in effect, "Who am *I* and how am I *distinct* from those people, relationships, and their expectations of me?" By the end of the second year, with the blossoming of language, the question manifests itself in the stage parents call "the terrible twos," which is really the beginning of a lifelong quest for balance between attachment and individuation.

Theories about the self are almost as old as the field of psychology: about 100 years. From the early writers like James (1890), Cooley (1902), and Mead (1934) to Maslow (1954) and more recently Loevinger (1976) and Kegan (1982) as well as the school of psychoanalysis called "self psychology" (Kohut, 1971; Galatzer-Levy and Cohler, 1993), virtually all theories understand the self as deriving both from a person's dependence upon "significant others" and his or her need to differentiate from those others. In other words, one needs to be *both* a separate person *and* a member of the family/group/community/profession/organization.

In one of the seminal papers in the field of family therapy, Bowen (1972) wrote of his struggle to differentiate from his own family, which happened to own a business. Bowen was the only sibling who had not stayed or returned home to work in the business. Although successful in his career as a psychiatrist, he found himself unable to avoid being drawn into his family's conflicts surrounding their business roles and their failure to grow as individuals.

Too much self-differentiation would not be adaptive for human development. We are a social species, and the family is our basic economic and cultural unit. It is the molecule. Just as molecules are composed of atoms, families are composed of individual people; but it is the structure and nature of the bonds connecting those people, and the dynamic forces operating among them, that make them who they are. Furthermore, what constitutes a "healthy" balance between individual differentiation and family cohesion varies across societies and across cultures within a society—a fact we shall need to keep in mind in the section on treatment, below.

On the other hand, too much resistance to differentiation is equally maladaptive. Without the freedom and without the support of one's family to pursue individual talents and dreams, creativity and growth are stifled. Conflict becomes chronic. People lack the flexibility to keep up with changing demands of their economic environment. For that reason alone, a business that serves the function of retarding its owners' development is not one whose family ownership continuity should be encouraged.

What is success? Confining ourselves to inter-generational family enterprise, let us define "success" in the long run, if and when:

1.   Both generations feel that the younger generation has made significant contributions to the business;

2.   They *either* passed the baton or made a good decision to sell the business, in which case they worked together to maximize its value;

3.   The *process* of getting there was personally rewarding for them, individually as well as collectively; and

4.   There were no serious personal casualties along the way.

An example of failing to meet the first criterion would be a family whose business never serves as a place where children can be validated as adults and appreciated by their parents. The second type of failure might characterize a business whose equity value was held down by a history of poor teamwork, poor leadership, or poor management of this family resource. An example of the third type of failure is where financial success has been achieved at the expense of the members' personal satisfaction, enjoyment of their relationships, or their moral values. The fourth type of failure could be found in a family business that made its owners and most of their children happy, but which contributed to one member's arrested development, chemical dependence, or other form of lifelong alienation.

The families that I would call addicted to their business have failed in most, if not all four, of those criteria.

A set of cases

My prior training and experience tends to attract more than my share of clients whose family firms are in crisis, or who want to avert an impending crisis. Hence I wouldn't claim that the number of families I see, in which members of the second generation are trapped in the business to their detriment, is a representative number; only that such cases are not rare.

At the time of writing I have had consulting engagements with 64 two-generation family business cases of sufficient duration to categorize them. (This excludes corporate management teams, non-family business partnerships, single-generation owners and some members of two-generation families who consulted me briefly or without including other key members.) By the four criteria listed above, at the onset of consultation only about one quarter of those 64 business families appeared to be family relationship success stories. Table 3 indicates how many (over the course of, or following consultation) either achieved a promising succession to the next generation or made a decision they felt good about, to sell the business.

A cautionary note regarding the data in Table 3: The classification reflects the author's subjective evaluations rather than a blind coding scheme. Furthermore, many of these families are still in process of addressing their issues, either with me or with other kinds of advisors; some fled from addressing them as soon as they came to light; still others, I hope, made positive steps after I lost touch with them. Nonetheless, I present my "best guess" numbers as a stimulus to other consultants: In how many cases do I feel my efforts were successful? Table 3 answers that question for this consultant only. Again, I emphasize: It tells nothing about the population of all family firms.

Table 3. Classification of 64 Two-generation
Family Business Engagements

Type of Case	Consultant's Idea of Success	Results to Date
16 cases (25%) At least one capable business person in the successor generation, with the interests and ability to carry the company on AND basic trust among family members who work in the business	**Succession** Effectively planning toward business succession and eventual disposition of parental assets in a way that meets the needs and desires of both generations	12 of 12 cases (**100%**) made good progress toward succession. 4 unknown
26 cases (41%) At least one capable business person in the successor generation, to whom torch could be passed BUT one or more persons or relationships a significant obstacle to business or family teamwork	**Liberty and Succession** It's hard to imagine the family business functioning profitably OR harmoniously, unless the unhappy member is liberated from it in a fair and constructive way	7 of 22 cases (**32%**) made good progress toward "liberty and succession." At least 3 cases of catastrophic breakdown. 4 unknown
22 cases (34%) No capable manager(s) in the next generation, for the size and complexity of their business OR members' capabilities nullified by dysfunctional family relationships	**Sale** From the standpoint of family harmony and individual development, these families probably should sell their firms when the present generation is ready to retire	Only 2 of 19 cases (**11%**) made good progress toward planned sale to employees or outsiders. At least 8 cases of catastrophic breakdown. 3 unknown

Clearly, among those clients who had no crippling conflict when they sought my help as a transition planning facilitator, all of those I kept track of made good progress. I was less effective with families who in my own opinion needed to create an alternative path for one or more members because those members' unhappiness, lack of realistic preparedness, and/or symptomatic behavior created a serious detriment to the business team. About a third of that group achieved what seemed to me a healthy outcome for all members. I was *very* ineffective with parents whose best course of action (again, in my own opinion) was *not* to pass the torch to their children. Only two of those, so far, have decided not to do so—11 per cent.

To answer the more cheerful question expressed above, more than 40% of the cases (21 of 53 known) did make decisions—either succession or sale—to all members' satisfaction. However, from the 32 cases who remained stuck as their problems deteriorated, we can conclude that unhappy, poorly collaborating families show great resistance to altering their course, even when working with a consultant who candidly airs his doubts about their family business's prospects for succession to the next generation.

Regardless how skewed this particular sample may be, other consultants surely encounter such families. We therefore need a theory about how they got where they are and what keeps them stuck.

Individuation in entrepreneurial families

It is not correct to say that family business success depends on good differentiation. Anecdotal case reports and a very small amount of statistical evidence suggest that the two variables are positively correlated (e.g., Swogger, 1991; Kaye, 1992; Lansberg and Astrachan, 1994). Nonetheless, to infer from that fact a linear cause and effect (inadequate individuation leads to problems in the business) would be fallacious. Probably the direction of effects is the other way around. Lansberg (1996) breaks radically from the traditional view in our field (e.g., Friedman, 1991; Swogger, 1991) when he writes, "A successful family business may, in fact, delay the process of individuation." My suggestion is even more unsettling: Some people bring their offspring into a business or come to work with their parents *in order to retard* individuation.

Should we regard the child's individuation problem as an accidental byproduct of the economic organization? No, because the family is a social system. What looks like an accidental result is, I believe, the dysfunctional system's *purpose*. Individuation is a problem for these families because parents brought children into a business *hoping (perhaps unconsciously) to delay their individuation*. Table 4 shows where I agree and disagree with the family business literature's view of individuation.

Table 4. Systemic Relationship between Individuation and Family Business Conflict

Accepted Wisdom *(mix of linear and systemic)*	*New Theory* *(systemic)*
1. Entrepreneurs by nature may have a tendency to be over-controlling as well as ineffective at building children's self-esteem, confidence, etc. On top of that, running a business sometimes leads parents to neglect children's needs for individuation.	1. People who are uncomfortable with individuation in their children's development find the prospect of bringing them into a business particularly attractive. They can use the family business system to maintain excessive cohesion or connections without actually meeting the young adults' developmental needs.
2. Whatever the causes of poor individuation, it creates problems when the next generation has to work together, resolve conflicts, pursue careers, choose leaders, etc.	2. The family shares rarely spoken fears about what might happen to its members and their relationships, if individuation is allowed to go too far. Conflict serves the function not of differentiating them but of locking them in problem maintenance cycles that protect them from the risks of change.
3. Above problems become obstacles to the parents' letting go. Added to the parent's own resistance to separating from the business, systemic resistance keeps the would-be successors underperforming and unempowered.	3. Same as accepted wisdom at the left
4. Most or all family members are unhappy with their lack of progress toward succession.	4. Most or all family members are relieved to maintain their painful but familiar equilibrium.

Step III in the two theories is the same systemic postulate; the process is circular, as the children's immaturity or inadequacy confirms the parent's low opinion of them. Step II in the old theory, however, is a linear cause-effect inference from the apparent correlation between individuation problems and family business problems. The new theory rejects that inference in favor of the key assumption that runs from step I through IV: Some families are so drawn to involve sons, daughters, and other relatives in their business that it looks as if they were *trying to prevent* healthy individual growth and family adaptation.

In systems theoretical terms: All open systems, including human social systems, assimilate energy and matter from their environment in order to maintain equilibrium with the energy they expend. Sometimes they change adaptively to resist entropy (resist breaking up and losing the informational value they bring to one another as a system). But systems don't always manage to do that. Sometimes the demands of the environment are greater than their capacity for adaptation, so they try to stave off destruction by rigidly resisting change.

Differentiation is an aspect of ego development. (*Ego* is the internalized capacity for self regulation as well as the experience of oneself as a whole person). It is not just a psychoanalytic concept; other disciplines give it the same importance under different names. For example, the philosopher Macmurray (1957) discussed the development of a self as agent rather than just an object to others. There is a developmental progression, from primitive aims and primitive forms of attachment to others, toward the balanced attachment and higher aims of the individuated self (Maslow, 1954; Loevinger, 1976; Vaillant, 1977; Kegan, 1982). Vaillant showed that the types of defenses people use can be hierarchized and correlated with a broad range of success measures. All the classic authors on the subject of self or ego development (all the way back to James, 1890) agree on a developmental hierarchy. An individual's primitive aims include *seeking to belong* to, and support, norms of the group; whereas *self-actualization* is a higher, more developed aim. Similarity to and connection to the group provides the necessary condition for development, but:

> It largely is differentiation from others that challenges and determines our activity....It is as if each individual felt his significance only by contrasting himself with others. (Simmel, 1950 translation)

Of course, all those classic authors were western, mostly American, authors. Self-actualization is an American concept, and it could be argued that we "baby boomers" and our children are excessively preoccupied with it. This article does not consider other cultures; but even if the balance point between individuation and attachment motives is shifted for different cultures, both motives exist: The need to find the right balance is universal in human development. Within every set of cultural norms, some families find a more comfortable balance than others.

Ego development, individuation, and addiction to the business

Table 3 indicates that among the 48 clients who, I felt, needed to liberate at least one member (if not the whole next generation) from the business, at least two-thirds have not managed to do so—or have managed not to do so. What long-term family processes made their business entanglement more like an addiction than a pleasure?

We must probe a little further into developmental psychology for a theory about causal processes in families that will eventually become "stuck" in the family business.

I have said that the symptoms of family business dependence are similar to those of chemical dependence (Table 1) and that their etiology is similar (Table 2). Chemical dependence begins first with a reason to use the drug—peer pressure, a way to avoid dealing with something, or both. Gradually, tolerance (the required dose) and dependence increase. So it is with family business dependence: It begins with either family pressure or avoidance of challenges outside the family, or both. Then tolerance (the level of rewards or privileges needed from the business in order to believe oneself satisfied) increases. The young person becomes trapped in the business, as doors to alternative career paths close.

It is easy to understand what motivates sons or daughters (or in-laws) whose parent, through a combination of overt and subtle messages, and perhaps a financial package they can't refuse, pressures them to come work in the business. But *what motivates the parent?* A desire to give his children wonderful opportunities? Surely that is part of it, but the opportunities are so narrowly defined that one suspects a more selfish motive. Is it just the need for trustworthy help, the fear that non-family managers will steal from him? Sometimes. Often, however, a motive seems to be that of keeping children and grandchildren close, or bringing them back home after an experimental period of living too far away.

If any of those essentially selfish motives is at work, we have to postulate poor ego development on the parent's part. Permission for a child to differentiate into a healthy, secure individual requires ego development on the part of his or her parents. They have to let go.

In other cases, it is not the parent but the child who instigates and presses to come into the business, overcoming parental reservations. The "employer of last resort" scenario happens when the son or daughter has failed elsewhere, or withdrawn in fear of failing. Severe lack of self-esteem can often be traced back to childhood, when parents didn't do all they could to build the child's confidence in his or her ability to make it in the outside world.

It should be pointed out that self-esteem varies, to some extent, congenitally; although parents affect it, children aren't equally easy to equip with self-esteem. Let us concern ourselves here, however, with those parents who did significantly less than they could have done for their children's self-esteem before those children ever came to work in the business. Again we would postulate poor ego development on the parents' part. Not all adults are whole enough (mature enough or "big enough") to devote themselves to building individuated self-esteem in their children. Some need to keep the children dependent and relatively undifferentiated.

This leads us to a testable theory: "Prisoners" or "addicts" of the family business—sons, daughters, in-laws who stay in the business despite being manifestly unhappy, unsuccessful, locked in chronic conflict, and perhaps ungrateful—not only have low self-esteem and inadequate adult differentiation from their families, they also have parents or parents-in-law with poor ego development who *resisted* the children's differentiation.

Unfortunately, I have found no literature on ego development among entrepreneurs. The theory outlined in Table 4 (right hand column) suggests a hypothesis: If consultants could do a family audit, assessing the parents' ego development, we ought to be able to predict the success of their family business succession. In other words, I would hypothesize that my clients' fates as indicated by the different cells of Table 3 might have been predicted by a good test of the parents' ego development.

Is individuation only an issue for children in family firms? No. It is an issue in normal development that seems to be especially difficult in this context. We all work on our relationships with our parents all our lives, but the family business can force a risky degree of overlap. When the performance pressure never ends, it is harder to balance love and duty against individual self-actualization.

Implications of the developmental theory

Let me summarize the implications of this argument, before turning to the treatment perspective.

1. Individuation is necessary for family business transition in Western societies. (Family business is as old as *homo sapiens*, whereas individuation is especially

problematic in modern times and in America. Healthy members of any society must individuate to a considerable degree, but we also suffer from the myth of individualism, which glorifies excessive autonomy and denies the primacy of teamwork, organizations, and families.)

2. Family business systems, by their nature, run the risk of overly resisting individuation.

3. Such resistance leads to conflict, which increases fears about individuation.

4. Unfortunately, the resistance may be justified, because individuation may well endanger family business transition.

5. Only those family businesses that don't *have to* do so will succeed over generations. In other words, families whose members had other paths on which they could have succeeded are the only ones with the capacity to thrive in business together over generations.

6. Many of those that *cannot* pass their enterprises successfully to the next generation are those families that can least afford not to—because their children are ill equipped for success elsewhere.

7. The role of a family therapist as family business consultant should not be to increase the number of families engaged in succession but to *narrow* the number to just those for whom healthy reasons to be a family business outweigh the unhealthy motives.

The mission of the Family Firm Institute and the mission statements of many firms serving owners of closely held companies explicitly or implicitly suggest that their purpose is succession for the sake of succession. Indeed, the words *success* and *succession* are often used synonymously. We say we abhor tax-driven planning, yet we are guilty of a comparable blindness: Our avowed mission seems to be succession driven rather than health driven. Instead, we should be in the business of helping entrepreneurs discover whether their overlapping family and business roles yield more advantages than disadvantages (Tagiuri and Davis, 1982). And we should be helping families liberate themselves from the fear of differentiation (Kohut, 1971; Pinsof, 1995).

Treatment

The foregoing sections have pointed out the strong resemblance between dysfunctional family business systems and the process of addiction, and explained how a family's business can become its drug.

Such a perspective may seem pessimistic, yet I arrived at it after enjoying ten years of satisfying work with business-owning families. Even the 50% of my clients who still have serious problems have usually accomplished some changes we can both feel good about.

Thus I feel positive about most of the people who are in family businesses, and optimistic about new prospects. The reason I can feel so optimistic about the outcomes of their work with me is that I don't try to help them improve their relationships *so they can stay in business together*. More often than not, the healthiest outcome is for the family business to assist at least one member, if not all of them, into the career equivalent of a recovery program.

The treatment model for an alcoholic family may be the most appropriate model to use with many family firms. Like alcoholic beverages, family business isn't poisonous if taken in moderation. In fact, family enterprise was the normal means of survival during our species evolution and for most of human history, and still is the norm outside the industrialized countries. But, like alcohol dependence, once it becomes symptomatic, it has to be regarded as a pathology: *No other problems will be treatable if the addiction is ignored.*

Just as an alcoholic family needs to be told that their concern (for example) about one child's school failures or eating disorder cannot be constructively addressed until they face the truth about the parent's addiction, so a family business consultant needs to tell his or her clients that their desired succession planning would be a waste and a sham if they refuse to face the painful truth regarding codependencies, self-defeating expectations of entitlement, addictive obsessions with work, lying or grandiose fantasies about the future. Unless their business represents a healthy life for the successors, the family business consultant is like a bartender, listening sympathetically to the drunkard's tale of woe while continuing to "serve" the system. Untreated addictions are progressive and fatal.

Readers familiar with the Jellinek chart, mentioned earlier, will recognize that Table 5 corresponds verbatim to the other side of that chart, which shows the challenging climb to recovery.

The treatment process is difficult, frustrating, and not always successful, but its chances are better with the following guiding principles:

Be aware of the risk factors. The earlier a consultant can recognize the risk factors listed in Table 2, the better his or her chances of helping to shift the family system to a course of recovery.

Table 5. Phases of Recovery (Individuals or Whole Family)

1. "Hits bottom"	
2. Acknowledgment	Honest desire for help
	Learns addiction can be arrested
	Leaves the business
	Awareness of spiritual emptiness
3. Realistic thinking	Sees possibilities of new way of life
	"Regular nourishment taken:" explores new sources of personal satisfaction
	Diminishing fears of unknown future
	Self-esteem returns (or begins)
	No more desire to escape
	Natural rest and sleep
	Family and friends appreciate efforts
4. Appreciation	New circle of stable friends
	New interests develop
	Application of real values
	Increased emotional control
	Care of personal appearance
	Therapy and group support continue with increased insight on past
	Enlightened and contented personal identity

Respect the people, not the business. Don't assume that our job is to save the family business. Help clients examine whether it is playing a healthy role in their lives. If not, then a successful outcome may be to get one or more members *out* of the business; possibly to help the whole family see ending their business relationships as something other than "failure." Whether they stay in business or not, it is our job to help them explore all their options more realistically.

Don't pathologize enmeshment. A lack of differentiation, or a high degree of individual subordination to the needs of the family, isn't necessarily dysfunctional. In a way it's like sexuality: What goes on between consenting adults in the privacy of their homes is no one else's business. As a consultant, therefore, one cannot assess family business health based on some sort of individuation score. The concept should be applied only where people experience unhappiness and frustration in their family business. Person A may be less individuated from her family than person B is from hers; but suppose A is happy with her life. Suppose it is culturally appropriate, in her world, to build an identity within rather than beyond the family of origin; suppose it suits her personality. B's level of individuation, though greater than her neighbor A's, may be frustrated by a family system that endorses the individualistic society's messages about achievement but at the same time, dysfunctionally, sabotages the individual's attempt to reach out for it. Only in B's case, not in A's, is there reason to consider the family business *possibly* an unhealthy environment.

Don't diminish the crisis. It created the motive and opportunity for radical change. Keep a sense of urgency, to achieve the clients' sincere recognition of their enmeshment in a codependent system. Challenge their denial. They have to want to help themselves; refuse to continue lying to themselves, each other, and others; and be willing to undergo pain. Schaef and Fassel discuss "the myth that rules will alleviate the disease of the addictive system." (1988) One of the quotations from their book earlier in this paper raises the disturbing question whether we as consultants sometimes urge mission statements, rules, and structures *codependently*—in our own misguided attempt to create the illusion of control.

Family members will want to avoid painful historical and emotional questions about what led them down destructive paths in the first place. They will prefer to make small changes in working roles. Often small changes *are* the best steps toward resolution, but sometimes they are only Band-Aids over infected wounds or internal hemorrhages. Keep alive the question whether being part of the business is really good for each member—until that question is definitely answered.

This is not to say that goals, mission statements, and rational procedures are bad things to urge on our clients. They may be important diagnostically, to see if the system is capable of implementing consistent rules. They seldom, if ever, constitute the whole cure.

Reframe the problem. When offering opinions, be sure they don't sound like judgments, which would only elicit defensiveness. It is crucial not to stigmatize people. If parents' personality defense mechanisms or entrepreneurial obstinacy have led to family problems, recognize that their conscious intentions were good. They have also led to business success.

It also helps to point out how widespread these problems are in our society. *Many* people have made the understandable human error of hiring a family member in hopes of giving that person a new start; or of forming a business partnership in hopes of turning a bad relationship into something better. Many people have walked the recovery road, too, with great success.

Create a safe environment for change. Take responsibility for the consultation, not for the outcome. Our responsibility is to create conditions for system members' constructive discourse about their concerns. If their discussion leads to anyone's leaving the business, they will need a safe context for dealing with that, too. (Just as we expect severe withdrawal symptoms in a person recovering from chemical dependence, it's not too far-fetched to view withdrawal from the business as an equivalent to detoxification.)

You're not telling them anything they don't know. You merely give voice to *the message the clients came to you to hear an expert say.* Say what has to be said about the course they are on, even if it is sad or frightening to contemplate.

Don't be the rescuer. As White and Whiteside (1995) admonished consultants who work with alcoholic families, beware of system pressure on the consultant/therapist to become the over-responsible, controlling counterfoil to the out-of-control, under-responsible members. Our clients' respect for our knowledge and expertise is seductive because we want to be heroes; that aspect of our personalities drew us into our professions in the first place. But rescuing others, even if it were possible, *dis*empowers them. We are not in charge of their lives.

They will need other support (peer and professional). Recovery is a process, not a quick fix. Therefore, giving up the addictive agent—in this case, the family business—is only a first step for the family member or members involved. The consultant who facilitates that step, like one who facilitates an alcoholism intervention, need not be the same one who will do the follow-up counseling. But it surely is our job to do everything possible to get the "recovering" client into an ongoing relationship with a career counselor, therapist, self-help group, or whatever appropriate resource will remain in touch with the course of recovery.

Behavior change will not be enough without increased understanding. Just as an addict needs to explore and develop a personal story ("why I'm an addict," "what my addiction has done for me as well as to me"), so our clients will need cognitive change. Be skeptical about action decisions that are reached too quickly.

Substitute healthier habits. The good news is that when family business is an addiction, it is a process addiction (like bulimia, or gambling) rather than a substance addiction like alcoholism. It is curable, not just treatable. The cure is to substitute healthier habits, in this case a new career for the individual or a new way of defining their identity as a family.

Conclusion and Warning

Most patients treated for process addictions (along with their family systems) do recover. As Table 5 suggests, the recovering family business system or recovering individual family business member can usually move on to a better life as an individuated person. They don't pine for the conflicts and anxieties of the former life in their family business.

On the other hand, in one important way the family business sickness is more dangerous than other addictions: The family business addicts' world is attractive and rewarding to the consultant. The same money that can seduce a young person away from her own independent career path and personally fulfilling lifestyle may also co-opt a consultant into affirming his client's self-deluding beliefs and self-destructive denial system. It is not only legal and financial advisors whom I challenge to consider whether the pecuniary attractions of their clients sometimes lead them to feed rather than confront that denial system. Even those of us who act as therapists, with years of clinical family therapy experience, can easily fall into the trap of treating the family business as our wealthy "patient" whose life is precious. In cases when a business is not the patient but the sickness itself, that is inexcusable.

References

Bork, D. (1986). *Family Business, Risky Business*. New York: AMACOM.

Bowen, M. (1972). On the Differentiation of Self in the Family. In Bowen, M., *Family Therapy in Clinical Practice* (pp. 467-528). New York: Jason Aronson.

Carroll, R. (1988). Siblings and the family business. In Kahn, M. and Lewis, K., eds., *Siblings in Therapy: Life-span and Clinical Issues* (pp. 379-388). New York: Norton.

Cooley, C. (1902). *Human Nature and the Social Order*. New York: Scribner's

Dashew, Leslie. (1995). Personal communication.

Herz Brown, Fredda (1994) Personal communication.

Friedman, S. (1991). Sibling relationships and intergenerational succession in family firms. *Family Business Review*, 4(1), 3-20.

Galatzer-Levy, R. and Cohler, B. (1993). *The Essential Other: A Developmental Psychology of the Self.* New York: Basic Books.

Hubler, T. (1995) "Obstacles to family change: our role in discovering them, naming them, and working with them". Paper presented to the conference on Psychosocial Dynamics of Family Business, Evanston, Illinois.

James, W. (1890). *The Principles of Psychology* (Vol. 1). New York: Holt

Kaye, K. (1985). Toward a developmental psychology of the family. In L'Abate, L., ed., *Handbook of Family Psychology and Therapy* (Vol. I, pp. 38-72). Homewood: Dow Jones-Irwin, 1985.

Kaye, K. (1991). Penetrating the cycle of sustained conflict. *Family Business Review*, 4(1), 21-44.

Kaye, K. (1992). The kid brother. *Family Business Review*, 5(3), 237-256.

Kaye, K. (1994). *Workplace Wars and How to End Them: Turning Personal Conflicts into Productive Teamwork*. New York: AMACOM.

Kegan, R. (1982). *The Evolving Self.* Cambridge: Harvard University Press.

Kohut, H. (1971). *The Analysis of the Self.* New York: International Universities Press.

Lansberg, I. (1996). *Managing Succession and Continuity in Family Companies.* Cambridge: Harvard Business School Press.

Lansberg, I. and Astrachan, J. (1994) Influence of family relationships on succession planning and training: The importance of mediating factors. *Family Business Review*, 7(1), 39-60.

Leibowitz, B. (1986). Resolving conflict in the family owned business. *Consultation*, 5(3), 191-205.

Loevinger, J. (1976). *Ego Development*. San Francisco: Jossey-Bass.

Macmurray, J (1957). *The Self as Agent.* London: Faber and Faber.

Maslow, A. (1954). *Motivation and Personality.* New York: Harper and Row.

Mead, G. H. (1934). *Mind, Self, and Society.* Chicago: University of Chicago Press.

Messervey, John. (1996) Personal communication (letter to author).

Pinsof, W. (1995). "An integrative problem centered approach to family business problems." Paper presented to the conference on Psychosocial Dynamics of Family Business, Evanston, Illinois.

Schaef, A. and Fassel, D. (1988). *The Addictive Organization.* New York: Harper-Collins.

Simmel, G. (1950). *The Sociology of Georg Simmel.* tr. and ed. by Kurt Wolff. New York: Free Press.

Swogger, G. (1991). Assessing the successor generation in family businesses. *Family Business Review,* 4(4), 397-411.

Tagiuri, R. and Davis, J. (1982) Bivalent attributes of the family firm. Working Paper, Harvard Business School. Reprinted 1996, *Family Business Review,* 9(2), 199-208.

Vaillant, G. (1977). *Adaptation of Life.* Boston: Little, Brown.

White, C. and Whiteside, M. (1995) "Alcohol and the family business: An uneasy partnership." Presentation to the Family Firm Institute, St. Louis.

§

IN 1994 the American Management Association published *Workplace Wars: Turning Personal Conflict to Productive Teamwork*, detailing the systematic approach I adapted from family therapy to resolve work group conflicts.

I use Plan A to Plan E, summarized here, as a mental flow chart when I'm working with family business conflict. The article also includes a diagram expressing how trust is a mutual process, as discussed more fully in "How to Rebuild Business Trust." Experience leads a relationship to become more or less trusting.

§

Conflict as Opportunity for Change*

Every business in the world has its share of conflict among employees, or between divisions, or with customers, suppliers, and governments. Who needs to add family conflict? Most of us try to avoid conflict, most of the time. It's uncomfortable, and the financial as well as emotional costs can be enormous. In fact, almost all the reasons one frequently hears for *not* bringing family members into firms center on the fear of conflict.

However, conflict is part of life. Stepping around it doesn't make it go away. The more we avoid conflict in business relationships, the more destructive it becomes. Business owners need to become so comfortable with their skills for addressing interpersonal problems productively, that they actually welcome the opportunity conflict offers for change. With a good conflict-resolving system, family business relationships become assets rather than liabilities, because they provide additional motivation for shared problem-solving.

Conflict well resolved is the life blood of growth and adaptation to change, in organizations of all kinds. The family business, however, has unique features that make conflict resolution more challenging:

Dual relationships: members can't negotiate in their business roles without ramifications for their family ties to one another. Furthermore, each one has a different set of family ties. They belong to different, but overlapping constituencies. For example, Joe represents the sales side of the business; the interests of all the in-laws; the males in his generation; his mother-in-law's branch of the family, etc.

Long histories: members' responses to one another are loaded with memories (including unconscious ones) going back to their childhoods and even to historical events two or three generations earlier.

---

* reprinted by permission from Family Business Network *Newsletter* No. 14, April 1996.

Unspoken agendas: many of the issues are difficult to talk about, for fear of hurting each other's feelings. In some family cultures, a motive like protecting one's inheritance, or an emotion like anger, fear, or envy would be morally incorrect.

Such factors in a family business only make systematic conflict-resolving skills more essential. For example, in our consulting work we use a kind of road map or flow chart.

A Conflict Resolving System

♦ Plan A: bring together all those who are involved in the conflict or might be involved in its solution, and get them to focus on their goals. The crisis has amplified theiir differences; sometimes hearing one another articulate shared goals reminds them to look for win/win outcomes together.

♦ Plan B, when Plan A is insufficient: clarify the differences and sort them into different categories. Some are merely misunderstandings, cleared up by active listening. Some are valuable differences of perspective (gender, for example; or generational) which should be turned into an organizational strength rather than a communications obstacle. Some differences are irrelevant to the shared goals, and simply need to be accepted. A few are truly fundamental conflicts that must not be ignored.

A leader—whether of the business or the family—can probably implement Plans A and B without a consultant. Plans C and D, however, may require a third party's perspective and professional aid.

♦ Plan C: members make formal commitments to change behavior, or to take specific responsibilities.

♦ Plan D: analyze chronic patterns of dysfunction. This requires consultation; despite some best efforts, interpersonal problems keep recurring. But not all conflicts are of that type, which is why this five-step system begins with the least intrusive, briefest interventions and only becomes more elaborate if and when necessary.

Resolving chronic conflict within systems of people has nothing in common with settling disputes between unrelated parties (for example, two corporations litigating a breach of contract). The goal of the latter is to *end* the relationship, whereas the goal within an organization is to *improve* relationships. Nowhere is this more vital than in a family business. Therefore, even when the conflict is a long-standing one, it is worth going through the travail of Plan D before giving up.

♦ Finally, Plan E: unilateral change on the part of individual members. Any one of them can empower him or herself to stop contributing to the problem, to take responsibility for their own actions, to improve communications even when others do their worst to obstruct it.

At each step, before tackling unresolved problems at a deeper level, leaders or facilitators have to gauge whether the relationship is worth the cost and trouble of saving it. Are certain crucial ingredients present, such as respect, affection (do they like each other?), economics (do they add value to each other's work?), and basic trust?

Trust: Impaired and Repaired

The most crucial—and fragile—element required is trust. What do you do when you begin to feel distrustful of someone? It's natural to withdraw from the relationship, put up a wall against further vulnerability, and blame the other person. Such defensive reactions make the problem worse. Instead, you need to assess three different areas of trust: honesty, intentions, or competence. You may be able to use a foundation of good trust in one or two areas, to build mutual trust in the problem area.

Figure 1. Trust as a gradual, reciprocal process: Mutual experience leads a relationship to become more or less trusting.

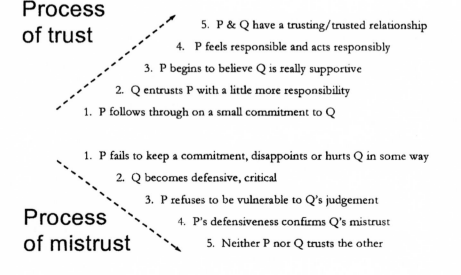

Process of trust

5. P & Q have a trusting/trusted relationship
4. P feels responsible and acts responsibly
3. P begins to believe Q is really supportive
2. Q entrusts P with a little more responsibility
1. P follows through on a small commitment to Q

1. P fails to keep a commitment, disappoints or hurts Q in some way
2. Q becomes defensive, critical
3. P refuses to be vulnerable to Q's judgement
4. P's defensiveness confirms Q's mistrust
5. Neither P nor Q trusts the other

Process of mistrust

The diagram shows that trust is a relative thing. It's not a matter of trusting someone absolutely. It's a process. Experience leads to either more and more trust (the up-sloping arrow), or more and more mistrust (the down-sloping arrow). It is a *reciprocal* relationship. If you don't trust me, that in itself is a reason for me to be somewhat less trusting of you—because you're going to be guarded in relation to me. This reciprocity means that we should speak of a *trusting/trusted relationship* rather than saying that any individual is either trustworthy or not.

As the diagram indicates, when person P keeps a commitment to person Q, Q's trust in P increases. P, reinforced by that fact, becomes even more responsive, responsible, hence trustworthy to Q. On the other hand, if P disappoints Q, Q is likely to defend against further disappointment by becoming more judgmental and less trusting. The effect on P? Defensiveness in the face of Q's criticism; thereby justifying Q's mistrust, and reciprocating it.

Conclusion

Conflict is **unavoidable** and **good** for a healthy family business. A conflict-resolving system is essential for any business team, but especially so where family issues and organizational issues intersect.

Members of the family business must recognize when interpersonal problems are important, and must have the skills (and *know* that they have the skills) to resolve them together.

Trust is an inherent part of teamwork. Assessing trust is crucial to a systematic process of resolving conflicts, because the process makes demands on participants' time, energies, and emotions. Sometimes it just isn't worth it, because something would have to change that is not going to change.

The process of building trust takes time. So does learning to address conflict forthrightly instead of evading it.

The real goal of conflict resolution programs is not just to resolve a particular problem but to change the team's or whole organization's culture. The most effective companies don't just have systematic conflict-resolving skills—they are conflict resolving systems.

§

I HAD DISCUSSED trust as an interaction process (not a static quality, present or absent) in my book *Family Rules* (1984) as well as in *Workplace Wars* (1994). The former is about family relations, not about business; and the latter is about organizational conflict, not particularly about family firms. In 1995, I noticed something simple and remarkably useful about trust and mistrust: It helps if family members clarify whether their statement "I don't trust X" is about the person's honesty, or about his or her motives, or about particular abilities.

Kaye, K. *Family Rules.* New York: Walker, 1984. Revised edition, St. Martin's, 1990. Republished: iUniverse, 2005.

Kaye, K. (1994). *Workplace Wars and How to End Them: Turning Personal Conflicts into Productive Teamwork.* New York: AMACOM.

§

How to Rebuild Business Trust

Mutual trust is indispensable to people who need one another in order to stay in business. When it breaks down, the only alternative to ending the relationship is to rebuild it "brick by brick."

WHAT MISFIRING of family circuits could possibly lead sons to stage a boardroom coup against a father, as in the Shoen family of U-Haul? What lifelong process of decay could turn a relationship so rotten that a father mounts a similar coup against his CEO son, as did Herbert Haft of the Dart Group? Differences over business policy cannot account for the feuds we hear about in some family companies. Nor are anger and hurt alone sufficient explanations.

Such enraged acts can only result when something vital to human life is injured: trust. Basic trust is the first thing an infant needs to learn—but the need never ends. Every adult's safety and emotional survival hangs on our ability to trust others as well.

That is one of the major reasons families exist. If I cannot trust my family, I am a lost soul. Normal, functional people who come to conclude that they cannot trust key family members feel understandably vulnerable and betrayed. No wonder some stop at nothing in their pursuit of justice—or revenge.

The one sentence I hear most often, as a consultant in the field of conflict resolution, is: "I don't trust him," or, "I don't trust her." It is truly a sentence: The persons being judged are sentenced to a purgatory from which they may never return, so far as their relationship with the speaker is concerned.

Nothing in life works without trust, especially in a family firm. The whole process of creating an enterprise that will survive its founder means entrusting it to others; and often one reason owners bring family members into their business in the first place is because they believe it will be easier to trust kin than non-kin.

> There are three kinds of trust: One has to do with honesty, another with intentions, a third with competence.

*   by permission of the publisher from Summer 1995 *Family Business* magazine, www.familybusinessmagazine.com

Unfortunately, a certain amount of distrust seems built into family firms. Entrepreneurs are often ambivalent about trust. The energy they needed to start their own business may have been fueled by their distrust of bosses they have worked for or resentment at some betrayal of trust by previous employers. Willing to risk capital, entrepreneurs trust their gut instincts—sometimes without due diligence. Yet studies of the entrepreneurial personality show that their instinct is basically to *minimize* risk. Thus they often zealously guard control and have difficulty trusting anyone else with business decisions. They may also have trouble believing in their children's ability to make successes of themselves, perhaps because, as business founders, they know so well the narrow margin between success and failure. So they use the business as a safety net for their offspring, which often turns out to be a snare.

It should not be surprising therefore that family business issues are all about trust, from the everyday problem of delegating responsibility to the ultimate doubt about whether the kids will try to put Grandpa out to pasture prematurely or stop visiting Grandma when she can no longer write a check. Unfortunately, one member's mistrust only breeds mutual mistrust and self-fulfilling prophecies about lack of trustworthiness in family members.

> Trust is always being built, tested, strengthened, or weakened. The Baileys should not regard their need to repair the bonds of trust as abnormal.

For example, consider the Bailey family and the packaging materials business that their grandfather started. John Bailey Jr., the founder's son, had retired from the business but remained chairman of the board. He was trying hard to turn the company's management over to his son John III and other members of the third generation. John III and his brother, Bill, were working in the business along with one of their two sisters, Sharon, and both sisters' husbands. But a breach had opened up between John III and Bill, on the one hand, and their sisters and brothers-in-law, on the other. It was steadily widening, threatening a breakdown in the business. (This actual family, whose names I've changed, is representative of many with whom I and other family business psychologists work.)

The problem was that the two sisters and their husbands didn't have confidence in either brother. John III, they said, was well-intentioned but lacked energy, vision, and communication skills. Bill—youngest of the four Bailey siblings—did possess those essential qualities of a president, but his sisters didn't trust him for another reason. "He throws money away," said Sharon. "And he's been known to lie."

So Sharon, the company's administrative vice-president, and her sister, Joanne, who was both a stockholder and the wife of the director of manufacturing, reacted the way most people do when they distrust others in vital relationships. They put up anticipatory defenses. Interpersonal "deterrents" of this kind recall the old nuclear arms race: They lead to escalated conflict and the threat of Mutual Assured Destruction. Each faction in the Bailey family blamed the other, defensively denying their own role in the breakdown of trust. Sharon and the brothers-in-law would call Dad long distance, complaining about John and Bill and undermining their decisions. Naturally, the brothers said *that* was the problem. Feeling besieged, the brothers used Sharon's "bad-mouthing and back-stabbing" as an excuse to ignore the substance of her complaints. When John acted with excessive authority, or when Bill "pulled one of his surprises" (in Sharon's words), they explained that they'd been reduced to operating that way in self-defense.

None of this helped the Baileys achieve their revenue goals as a team. It was a vicious circle. Mutual distrust bred the kind of behavior that justified further defensiveness and only eroded the Baileys' common bonds and goals. Yet trust is indispensable to a relationship in which people need one another, as the Baileys did, in order to stay in business. When trust is lacking or insufficient, the only alternative to ending the relationship is to rebuild it—contrary to the defensive instinct. In the words of another client, "We have to take down the wall brick by brick and use the bricks to build a bridge."

Three Types of Trust

The first step in trying to turn the Baileys' deteriorating situation around was to clarify the nature of the different members' distrust, for there are at least three kinds of trust. One has to do with honesty. Sharon did not believe she could trust her brother Bill, the regional sales manager, to tell her the truth. He had lied to her more than once, she said. "It seems to be his way of avoiding conflict. He doesn't want to tell me bad news, or he doesn't want to be criticized—so he tells me what he thinks I want to hear. When I find out the truth, I'm twice as upset as I would have been if he had been straight with me in the first place."

Another kind of trust has to do with intentions: Would this person knowingly hurt me? Both John and Bill had concluded that their sisters and brothers-in-law intended to unseat them, to reduce their power and their incomes as well. That was how they interpreted Sharon's frequent emphasis on accountability and performance reviews.

We devise tests of other people's trustworthiness, without telling them we're testing them. The Baileys realized that such games had gone too far.

The third kind of trust—or mistrust—is about competence. The faction of the family that was challenging John III's leadership didn't doubt his honesty or his good intentions, just his ability to lead the company. They had too much at stake to entrust it to a lackluster president. Sister Joanne explained, "The others [among her generation] don't know what to do with him. He can't manage people, and my husband says they all try to keep him away from important customers. His heart is in the right place, but his brain isn't."

Those three kinds of trust present similar challenges. In each case, a process over many years has built a wall of distrust. A dismantling and bridge-building process can begin, but it will take time. Trust will come only gradually.

In helping the Baileys begin that process, I saw hope in the fact that each person's concerns about other family members were limited to only one type of trust. If Sharon had seen her brothers as inept, lying scoundrels who intended to cheat her, I would have encouraged her to dissolve her business relationship with them. If either John or Bill had seen Sharon or their brothers-in-law as untrustworthy in all three ways, I would have held out no hope. (As important as the process of building trust is the assessment of whether the people you love and work with can *ever* merit your trust.) Instead, the brothers had positive things to say about Sharon's skills and her honesty. They only doubted her motives, because of the way she made trouble for them, "when she doesn't get her way." They didn't want a whole new sister, and they didn't want her out of the business; they just wanted her behavior to change. For her part, Sharon acknowledged the good motives of John and the business skills of Bill. Those elements of trust that did exist in the Bailey family gave us a foundation upon which to begin to repair their damaged relationships.

The second thing I pointed out to them was that in all human relationships—friendship, marriage, parent-child relations, teammates, customer-vendor, employee-manager, or business partnerships—trust is an on-going process. Trusting in other people's competence means giving them room to learn, and testing their competence one step at a time. I let my son drive first when I was in the car, then alone on short daytime errands, and only after that on his own. Trusting someone's honesty and good intentions is likewise a matter of experience. If your bank extends a $100,000 line of credit, it is relying as much upon your history of repayment as upon any collateral you put up. Trust is a process that requires collecting information (overcoming prejudice) over time; controls and risk assessment (distinguishing between those who can, and cannot, be trusted); feedback and evaluation ("I can trust him just so far, before I need to know the results").

Should trust be automatic in families? Absolutely not. In fact, the Baileys were dealing with a challenge every family faces: How do we allow our members to become individual adults with their own particular talents, lifestyles, and separate goals? That process is called individuation, and the life cycle of every

> Like our skin, trust normally gets scratched and bruised, and then heals. The key is to back up a step and reassess—"have I entrusted too much, or the wrong things, to this person?"—rather than overreacting and giving up prematurely.

healthy family involves a delicate balance between individuation and shared purpose. In a family business, allowing each member to develop as an individual is even more challenging, because everyone's livelihood depends on developing and maintaining a shared purpose. Individuation is a matter of how far the members will trust, tolerate, and even celebrate each other's uniqueness before their differences create anxiety over the possible risk to their interdependence.

When Sharon objected to Bill's lavish entertaining of customers, or when both brothers bridled at her insistence on accurate expense records and cost accounting, the issue was whether they could trust one another in their shared enterprise despite such differences in personal priorities. My job was to help them decide whether those differences might be more of a strength than a threat.

Building Trust

People continually reassess whether others should be trusted. The process is ongoing and normal. Therefore, the Baileys should not regard their need to repair the bonds of trust as abnormal or "dysfunctional." Trust is always being built, tested, strengthened, or weakened. Likewise, when mistrust has become rampant, as it had in the Bailey family, the approach to repairing it is really the same as the normal process of establishing mutual trust in any important relationship.

That word, *mutual,* was the next important idea the Baileys needed to grasp. Trust never works one way, not for long. It has to be a trusting-trusted relationship. If you don't trust Joe, is that a statement about Joe, or about something between you and Joe? It may be a statement about where your relationship with him is at that point in time.

Trust is a process that requires collecting information over time. Trusting in others' competence means giving them room to learn.

All of us are passengers in boats rowed by others. Each of us also rows a number of boats in which some of those same others are our passengers. Facing backward, the rower pulls the oars while the passengers helplessly eye the obstacles ahead. The passengers have a right to be scared. They are foolish if they have blind faith in the rower who says, "Sit back and trust me." Unfortunately, the natural anxiety resulting from our vulnerability in such circumstances leads people to play some risky games. We devise tests of others' trustworthiness, without telling them we're testing them. We discourage others from trusting us too much, often because we fear the responsibility of accepting their trust. We undermine trust between others if we fear that their good relationship jeopardizes our own relationship with one or the other. And, of course, we lie: We pretend to trust more than we do, and we pretend to be more trustworthy than we are.

The Baileys sought help because they recognized that such games were going too far. They were overreacting, escalating the distrust, and defining the other family members as hopelessly untrustworthy. Instead, all of the members needed to ask what they could do to earn the others' trust and to make the others more trustworthy—which turned out to be the same process.

I don't want to suggest that the Baileys' problem was solved simply by Sharon and the in-laws trusting her brothers more, and vice versa. John is still president of the company, but the board (the four siblings) narrowed his job description to better fit his skills and interests. This family now makes some decisions by executive committee, and shares some figurehead functions once done by their father alone. Sharon won the management performance reviews she had campaigned for—with at least a partial impact on individuals' bonuses—in exchange for stopping the "tattling" behavior that had so factionalized the family leaders.

The process of trust can go awry in many ways. Most of the time, erosion in the process can be reversed by backing up, understanding what is really being asked and said, and earning and giving trust gradually, by degrees. You can always bail out of the process, which means deciding not to be in the kind of relationship that requires trust. (For all I knew at the outset, any of the Baileys might have reached that decision in the course of our work.) But people who go through life withdrawing from challenging relationships too hastily, upon insufficient evidence, wind up just as bereft of mutually productive alliances as those who stay too long in destructive ones.

§

THE EDITOR of *Family Business Review* asked me to comment on an article by John Haynes and Thomas Usdin entitled "Resolving Family Business Disputes through Mediation" (1997). I found the authors' claims for the utility of mediation far too broad, as opposed to a family systems consulting approach.

§

Comment on Mediation*

THE ROLE AND POSSIBLE VALUE of mediation in family business disputes is much narrower than the authors claim. It is possible to do serious harm by trying to use that tool as the whole intervention. The Surgeon General of the Family Firm Institute should warn consultants who propose to do so that unless they are clinically trained and prepared to intervene in family dynamics and individual psychology, or unless their mediation is coordinated with concurrent family therapy by a qualified professional, they may expose themselves to accusations of malpractice.

Mediation does have a place. Its place is along a continuum of legal processes for the settlement of material claims in disputes, as shown in Table 1.

Aristotle first elucidated the structure and means of persuasion which mediators bring to disputes, in his *Rhetoric*, in the fourth century B.C. Mediation can be the optimal settlement process, as Table 1 indicates, in that it provides the structure of orderly rhetorical persuasion, benefiting from the experience of a trained third party, without giving an arbitrator control over the final resolution. The terms of their settlement remain with the parties themselves, as Haynes and Usdin explain and illustrate.

The key word, however, is *settlement*. Contrary to their article, the process is not at all concerned with the relationship between (or among) parties, but rather with a settlement of some kind—usually a financial one, though it may also involve custody of children or animals, visitation, participation rights in certain decisions—any settlement that allows disputants *to end or significantly reduce a relationship they hate.* Sometimes it does come to that in a family business. Cousins might need to draft rules for voting control over their family business or wealth management. Siblings who have found it impossible to work together need to agree on the formula for purchasing shares from those who are leaving the business. Or they may be disputing a non-compete covenant. Disputes like those, when resolved well, don't necessarily *preclude* later familial relationships;

---

*   *Family Business Review*, 1997, Vol. X, pp. 131-134. Reprinted with permission fromthe Family Firm Institute, Inc. All rights reserved.

but their material settlement goes nowhere near resolving the relationship problems. Mediation can at best function for damage control, to resolve a particular matter so that other aspects of a relationship, not under dispute, have a chance to survive.

That is entirely different from repairing or enhancing relationships, which has to happen if people are to work together more productively. I cannot agree in any way with the authors' assertion that mediation "provides the best opportunity for an equitable solution which preserves future relationships and leaves all sides essentially satisfied."

The anecdote offered by Haynes and Usdin as an occasion for mediation is not one, in my opinion. They claim that settling the family's financial and governance issues led to "restoration" of family relationships between the children and their father, and "the basis for a better relationship" with their stepmother. This is a startling assertion, which needs to be supported with evidence. Having no facts about the people they describe, I can only express skepticism. If a party of objective evaluators were to do an assessment one year after the mediation and conclude that indeed, it did lead to a better relationship, I'd count it a most atypical case. More consistent with our experience of family relationships would be that the disputants *at best* live by the terms of their settlement in strained mutual resentment for the rest of their lives. More commonly, they agree at the time, but long-standing unaddressed issues (hurt, rivalry, distrust) produce even greater hostility the next time conflict erupts.

In the case depicted, one should expect the son and daughter to have a long history with their stepmother as well as their father, of mutual grievances and distrust. The daughter may also be angry about having been trapped in the position of disputant over a business asset she plays no active role in. And the son, of course, has a whole set of issues with his father involving respect, empowerment, entitlement, desire for appreciation, responsibility *versus* desire for autonomy, and so on. Although the exercise of agreeing on a statement of the problem could play a role in framing the family's discourse if it were one intervention among several, the way this mediator framed it certainly didn't get to the roots of the problem. (Nor was the mediator really neutral to the parties: What right had she to require in advance that the father keep the business in his estate so that "the new wife would not be asked to give up any of her legal rights"?)

Table 1. Legal and extralegal processes for settling material claims in disputes.

	Negotiation	Mediation	Arbitration	Litigation	Violence
involvement of legal system:	no legal professional	usually an attorney		whole judicial system	cause for subsequent civil or criminal action
basis:	the parties' interests		rights	relative power	
decision control:	the parties themselves		expert third party	jury of peers	brute force
typical resolution:	win-win	minimize loss for both	win-lose	lose-lose	

How could the described mediation process have done any harm in this case? At least two ways occur to me, hypothetically. One is that by precluding discussion of the historical, emotional, developmental context of the animosity between children and stepmother, far from guaranteeing that all future debate be rational and constructive, the process may have guaranteed acting-out behavior by any or all members. Secondly, from the point of view of business succession, the mediator's simplification of the problem—how to keep the two firms symbiotically married—may or may not have been the best possible outcome from a profitability standpoint, let alone the family dynamics. (A psychologist would notice that Dad didn't stop at trading his wife in for a younger woman; he made the latter his son's counterpart in a second business.)

The authors begin their article by echoing the point that members of a family business usually don't want to end relationships; they need to make them better (Kaye, 1991). Unfortunately, they then assert without proof or plausibility that a technique designed only to minimize mutual destructiveness—to avert litigation or violence—has the power to reverse the misunderstandings and hurts of a lifetime. With similar optimism, medieval alchemists claimed they could turn dross into gold.

It would be tempting, but dangerous for a business owner or a consultant who is uncomfortable intervening in family conflict to believe in such an attractively simple course of treatment. What business owner wouldn't contract with the alchemist who offers to do in "about twenty hours" what others might spend forty or more hours on, in emotional meetings spaced out over months or even years? What financial or legal consultant to a family business wouldn't be interested in a few days of instruction in one technique that could justify the self-description "trained conflict resolver," without the necessity of five or more years of training and experience that a license to practice family therapy requires?

Caveat emptor applies, I suppose; and one's professional objection to the irresponsibility of others inevitably invites the charge of turf-guarding. But I caution consultants that mediation techniques are appropriate, at most, for the settlement of material issues. Family breakdown requires family therapy.

References

Haynes, J.M. and Usdin, T.M. (1997). Resolving family business disputes through mediation. *Family Business Review*, X(2), 115-134.

Kaye, K. (1991). Penetrating the cycle of sustained conflict. *Family Business Review*, IV (1), 21-44.

§

WE'RE LUCKY if we can make a few positive changes in ourselves. Hoping to solve relationship problems by convincing the other person to change is worse than a waste of time—it's a way of refusing to do the only constructive thing that might, if we're really determined, improve the situation. That is to try some different behavior ourselves, in hopes of getting a better reaction.

§

On Trying to Remake Others*

What can you do about a family member whose behavior at the office has become intolerable?

"DO PEOPLE EVER CHANGE?" It's the question I'm asked most frequently by frustrated members of family businesses. They may be referring to a sister's rigidity about policies and paperwork, or a brother-in-law's lack of respect for others' time. It may be Mom's explosiveness toward employees who don't measure up, or Dad's closed-mindedness.

Those who ask always seem to be stuck with a family member or key employee whose behavior has become intolerable. Some are hopeful that a psychologist might be able to cure the person, but on the whole, lay opinion seems to be: "No, people don't change; you have to just live with them or replace them."

Is that sadly true?

It cannot be absolutely true, because most of us clearly continue acquiring knowledge and skills all our lives. Take Walter, for example, a 35-year-old who's been working for ten years with his father, brother, and sister. All three of them say the same thing: Walter is the nicest guy in the world, but he can't keep a deadline of any kind, and he always has an excuse. They even know a label for Walter's behavior: "passive-aggressive."

Walter's learning didn't stop ten years ago. He is the computer literate member of the family. He flies hang gliders. He buys boat engines, which a division of the company rebuilds profitably thanks to Walter's continually growing technical expertise and market tracking.

During the years when his family has been bemoaning the lack of change in him, Walter has married and become a parent. Curiously, his wife seems not to have noticed the annoying pattern that drives his family nuts.

Walter's family expressed the question as one of personality: "Do passive-aggressive people ever change?" This implies that it isn't a matter of Walter

---

*   by permission of the publisher from Winter 1998 *Family Business* magazine, www.familybusinessmagazine.com

changing specific kinds of behavior. Can we change him into a whole different kind of person?

The answer to that is no. But can people change their attitudes and behavior? Of course they can, within limits, if they acknowledge they have contributed to the problem. People who are unfortunate enough to blame everyone but themselves for interpersonal problems are beyond treatment by any intervention known to the behavioral sciences. (I predict that the first psychologist to win a Nobel Prize will be whoever, in the next century, finds a cure for people who insist there's nothing wrong with them.) Will Walter acknowledge that his deadline failures and excuse-making in the family business are problematic behavior? Does he want to change?

We all have a range of behavior from which we select our customary responses to different situations. For example, people who are rude and belligerent when they feel threatened also have in their repertoires the ability to be patient and considerate. It's not that the person is incapable of considering others' sensitivities; it's just that he does so under some circumstances and not others.

An example would be the guy who is constantly making racially or sexually offensive "jokes." "That's just the way I am," he says to those who criticize him. The critics, however, might then ask: "Do you tell those jokes to your mother-in-law? To your minister's wife?" No, he admits, he doesn't, which proves that, when he wants to be, he can be selective about where and to whom he tells such jokes. The behavior is under his control.

I apply this principle when working with business partners who don't communicate well with each other, who are "bad listeners." Often these partners listen quite attentively when dealing with customers. Instead of trying to teach them whole new patterns of behavior, I learned to focus on the communication skills they routinely apply with customers. It's infinitely easier to coach people to extend their existing repertoire to new situations than it is to teach them entirely new forms of behavior.

People change in small steps, and they are unwilling to risk it unless they receive positive support from the family.

In Walter's case, the challenge would be to persuade him to be as responsible in his business relationships as he is with his wife and children. "I don't disappoint my wife," he freely admits, "because when I disagree with her I say so in the first place." When he's given an assignment he's not comfortable with in the business, however, he doesn't show the same assertiveness. He keeps quiet about it, and his resentment shows up in his attitude toward deadlines. Walter's task, then, is to learn to express his disagreements with family members openly, as he does with his wife.

People change in small steps. No one in her right mind is going to abandon all the defenses she has built up over years of experience—for example, with her siblings in the family business—merely because some therapist pinpoints her defensiveness as part of the problem. What she might do, though, is lower her defenses just a little in an area where the risk is small. Then, if her slightly greater openness meets with responses that are slightly more constructive—or more respectful, or more dependable, or less insulting—she may move in the direction of less defensiveness.

Walter's behavior is another kind of defense. He isn't going to abandon the whole strategy that has protected him for years. But he can watch for the occasion to test a different approach, in circumstances where the risks aren't too great and there's a chance family members might notice and appreciate the change. In order to encourage Walter to change, we have to give him a different aspect of ourselves to respond to.

Change needs to be gradual for another reason: If it isn't, the group is likely to undermine it. Everyone claims to believe in change, but this usually comes down to wishing that other people would change their obnoxious ways without substituting anything new. When it comes to positively supporting the changes their family members actually make, it can be another story. The reality is that families, like all human organizations, resist radical change more effectively than they promote it. "Better the devil ye know than the devil ye know not" seems to be a universal principle.

Finally, people change developmentally. They enter new stages of life with different agendas and concerns. They mature. A change in behavior that would be very difficult at age thirty, when a young adult is struggling to define his identity and individuality, may be easier at forty-five when the desire to rejuvenate hits him. More than one seventy-year-old who can't be convinced of anything has softened considerably by the time he reaches a ripe eighty.

When researchers say that personality is relatively stable over the life span, this only means that how Walter compares with other thirty-five-year-olds is similar to where he will stand relative to other forty-five-, fifty-five-, and sixty-five-year-olds as time goes by. It doesn't mean there isn't any change with age.

I have known many Walters who did change. One learned to recognize his habitual impulse to react "passive-aggressively," and, instead, to express his objections openly before accepting a commitment. Another eliminated his constant "kidding" put-downs of his wife and sisters. It isn't at all unusual for men and women whose eyes have been opened to the problems they are causing to start taking the initiative to communicate proactively, or dress more professionally, or take more responsibility.

So, although we therapists have no magic wands for changing personality, we are able to help the Walters of the world, if and when they acknowledge they contribute to the problem. We can help them extend their repertoire of effective social skills into domains and relationships where they have not chosen to use them in the past. We should expect them to change only gradually, however, taking small risks, testing the waters, and seeing what kind of responses they get from their families and co-workers before developing new habits. Finally, the degree of change they are capable of will depend on whether they have mastered the developmental challenges up to that point in their lives and achieved an appropriate level of maturity.

Those of us who toil in the realm of family dynamics have learned to push for slow, evolutionary shifts rather than a revolution in anyone's basic personality. No, a person doesn't change into someone else. But we can all stand a little refinement.

§

IN "When the Family Business is a Sickness," I revealed two harsh facts:

Of the families I had worked with who needed to liberate one or more members from the business before they could hope to pass it on successfully, only a third were able to let those family members go their own way.

Of those who probably should sell their business because they were either dysfunctional or didn't have anyone in the next generation capable of running it, almost none moved in that direction, notwithstanding my frankness.

In the following article, I reframed the point in more positive terms. The success of a family business should be measured by the opportunities it creates for the next generation, whether they choose to go on with that business or to follow their own dreams.

§

Happy Landings:
The Opportunity to Fly Again*

The success of a business for its owners is measurable in terms of the opportunities it creates for their beneficiaries. Perpetuating that business is only one of many possible opportunities for them.

REPORTEDLY as many as a quarter to a third of viable U.S. businesses remain in the same families from one generation to the next. That is a remarkably high number; not a poor record at all. Yet, if the vast majority of family businesses are not destined for that kind of transition, what are we experts doing for *them*? Are we doing a disservice by our almost obsessive focus on the succession process?

Too many families can't bring themselves to get *out* of a business when they no longer have capable and motivated leadership, or to get unsuited family members out of the business when their relationship with it or each other jeopardizes everything. I have written about chronic conflict (Kaye, 1991), about "prisoners of the family business" (Kaye, 1992), and about families' unhealthy relationships with business (Kaye, 1996). With due respect to the many healthy family firms, this article proposes a conceptual change, a research agenda, and a consulting orientation toward family functioning and *opportunity* rather than succession.

Family Business Success Means Opportunity Building

The ultimate success of a family business can be defined identically to the success of any parent: gauged by the *value added to next-generation opportunity*. Parents, by nature, want to find or create opportunities for their children, enabling the latter to start their adult lives with advantages over other young adults in the same society. That is why a common measure of how well parents have done is how

---

*   *Family Business Review*, 1998, Vol. XI, pp. 275-280. Reprinted with permission from the Family Firm Institute, Inc. All rights reserved.

much they have *increased* their children's socioeconomic standing, relative to where they themselves started two or three decades earlier.

This definition refers to opportunities created for all children in any family; regardless of gender, intellect, proclivities, or gifts. In the case of a business-owning family, it would apply to those who don't enter the business as well as those who do.

Successful parents may provide advantages of many kinds, including:

External Advantages
a profitable, already viable business
a professional degree
investment capital
a network of social connections
freedom

Internal Advantages
physical health
mental health and good judgment
positive self-esteem
moral principles and sound practices
technical know-how

Driven by biological instincts, most parents try to give their offspring as many of those competitive advantages as possible. Entrepreneurial success creates diverse opportunities, most of which are better accessed with cash (for postgraduate tuition, travel, investment, politics, philanthropy, financial independence, etc.) than by the inside track to a job in the family business. In short, family success does not necessarily entail retaining ownership of a business.

Confining the discussion to family enterprises in which the next generation does become active, Table 1 offers a perspective on success that transcends the question of succession.

From that perspective, successful consultation means liberating individuals or whole families from any of the failure conditions listed on the right side of Table 1, and maximizing their chances of achieving the full list of criteria on the left. If the business does stay in the family and/or if family members stay in the business, educators and advisors ought to do our utmost to ensure that we're really helping to transfer opportunity rather than its opposite: entrapment. That should be the responsibility of a family's legal and financial advisors as much as it is that of psychological advisers; especially since relatively few have psychological advisers, while nearly all have legal and financial counsel.

Table 1. Success Criteria and Corresponding Failures of a
Family Business

*Score success if **all** of the following are achieved:*	*Score failure if **any** of the following occurs:*
Both generations feel that the younger generation has made significant contributions to the business.	The business doesn't serve as a place where children can be validated as adults and appreciated by their parents.
They *either* pass the baton or make a good decision to sell the business, in which case they work together to maximize its value.	The equity value of the business is reduced by poor teamwork, poor leadership, or poor management of this family resource.
The *process* of getting there is personally rewarding for them, individually as well as collectively.	Financial success is achieved at the expense of the members' personal satisfaction, enjoyment of their relationship, or their moral values.
There are no serious personal casualties along the way.	The family business gives some of its owners and their children joy, but significantly contributes to other members' arrested development, chemical dependence, or lifelong alienation.

An example of consulting failure can be found in fifth-generation Hasbin Molding Co., controlled by the widow of the founder's grandson. Her two children, Buddy and Shirley, ran the company; each was divorced and had three adult children. Three of those six fifth-generation members were employed in the business, as well as the spouse of one. Buddy was the hands-on manufacturing vice president, which really meant plant manager. Shirley had the title of sales vice president, but she actually functioned as president in all respects but one: Neither Buddy nor his son, a machinist, took any direction from her.

Shirley's two sons were the company's principal salesmen. Although they worked hard, Buddy wasn't convinced of their worth. He cited numerous examples of how they were getting a "free ride." As if bent on proving their uncle's point, at the time our consultation began, the two young men had defied their grandmother by flying first class instead of coach on a business trip to Hong Kong. Shirley wasn't happy about her sons' flagrant disregard of company policy, but she was incensed about Buddy's accusations. He had bullied her as a child, his alcoholism had ruined family life, and he continued to be verbally abusive and demeaning despite ten years of sobriety. Buddy and Shirley agreed on almost nothing, the company was going nowhere, but Mrs. Hasbin refused to discuss selling it and refused to proceed with estate planning until her family proved they could work together harmoniously.

Buddy and Shirley did agree on one thing: There was no way they or their sons could work together in the future. I failed, however, to convince them that an assertive united front on that one point would more effectively persuade their mother than the power struggles that only served to maintain their problems. The company attorney, whose firm had doubled as Mrs. Hasbin's estate counsel, failed to use their 20-year relationship to budge her from her angry position. She feared that if she sold the company or allowed either Buddy or Shirley to exchange stock for other assets, she would lose her power over their paychecks and thereby her control over their unhappy lives and what little control she had over her grandchildren as well. That was true.

The Happy Landings Metaphor

In aviation, every aircraft is in the process of landing from the moment it takes off. The force of lift produced by motion of its wings through the air merely postpones its fall. The pilot's work is all aimed at bringing the aircraft down at the optimal place and time—instead of returning to Earth in a less desirable place, time, or condition. So with any human enterprise: The question is not whether it will survive in perpetuity but when, where, and how it will terminate. *How* is even more important than when and where: An unscheduled landing at an alternate airport preserves all the capital assets (financial, intellectual, and human), so they can be used again for another trip. An unrelenting effort to reach their planned destination may put safe alternates out of reach, and thus destroy all those assets.

The analogy may help to clarify what should be the job of family business educators, researchers, and consultants alike. It is to help owners recognize when the time comes to redirect or terminate their "flight." Sooner or later, every business-owning family (if not in this generation than in the next or the next), needs help looking for the best place, time, and manner to land safely.

Research Agenda

In order to fulfill that function responsibly, we need much better answers than we currently have, to two sets of questions.

The first set involves predicting where things are headed under various scenarios. I won't belabor the airplane analogy because, unfortunately, we experts on family business are closer to astrological forecasters than to aviators or scientists as yet. For example, when clients asked, "What happens if next-generation leaders of a family business try to share the CEO function equally among two or three siblings, in-laws, or cousins?" I used to say with as much expert authority as I could muster, "It won't work." More recently, I've heard myself saying, "It depends on a number of factors...." The bald truth would be, "I don't know." So, too, with questions about nonworking siblings' stock ownership, the importance of outside experience before entering the family business, the size of firms requiring a "real" board, and so forth.

Most of us realize that research on questions like those is currently insufficient. At least our young field has built the institutional support for such research, which may take another decade to reach a critical mass that one could call a genuine body of knowledge. The second set of questions, however, has barely begun to be asked; and I think they are just as critical.

This second set of questions deals with human beings' persistence in holding on to family enterprises that are clearly failing on the criteria of Table 1; enterprises that we can see *aren't* providing many external or internal advantages for the next generation and actually seem to be eroding their opportunities. There is a direct analogy to aviation psychology, because the latter field, too, has yet to discover the answer to this question: "What leads an intelligent, experienced (non-airline) pilot to fly on into worsening weather conditions when running out of fuel, fatigued, and with known equipment malfunctions?" From the point of view of human psychology, the answer in both domains may turn out to be the same.

Why the resistance to letting go—of unhappy family members, of the business itself? The author's consulting sample (Kaye, 1996, discussed below) shows how strong this resistance is. But why?

When patients are treated for a mental illness, their families, physicians, and health maintenance organizations expect to know the scientific basis for their particular diagnosis and treatment plan. In our field, there hasn't been any research at all, as yet, that could provide a scientific basis for saying, "Family business A has what it takes to pass to the next generation; Family B's problems are not fixable; Family C's problems can be solved by taking steps x, y, and z." Of course, we do make statements like those and we are often right—but we cannot long continue without a body of statistically valid research.

What we do have are some good theories about individual and family development, and some concepts that help us think about the resistance to letting go of a family enterprise that isn't working. We need to test those theories. Is it *true* that some families are afraid of individuation (Kaye, 1996)? *Individuation*, or the equivalent term *differentiation*, means that healthy family members allow each other and themselves to balance their shared identity with distinct separate identities and purposes that may sometimes take them in different directions without jeopardizing their family bonds.

Family business succession sometimes appears to be a means of resisting individuation—as though chasing a parent's dream were the only way to maintain family bonds. That, in turn, intensifies conflict, which increases fears about individuation; so the problem escalates. Unfortunately, the fears may be justified because individuation does endanger family business survival in any family business that happens to be built around stifling individuation. Will systematically gathered data support or disconfirm that good theory?

What role does ego development play in children's ability to make the break, or in parents' ability to accept it? For children to grow into healthy, secure individuals, their parents must have enough ego development to let them go.

Ego development means the ability to control internal instinctual reactions and anxiety, and the external stress of others' explicit demands and implicit expectations. Herbert's (1989) groundbreaking study of a select sample offers a model for personality studies of entrepreneurs and their families, which could be aimed at the questions raised here.

We need to know, too, what role social pressures play in people's difficulties about terminating family firms. Are there cultural variables that make some families define success in terms of business ownership and family participation? Surprisingly, films, novels, and theater have portrayed negative images for centuries—family business as an unhealthy trap, a spoiler of children, or a home for ne'er-do-wells. Why, then, do we still see so many families equating success with succession?

A research question for anthropologists, perhaps, is whether human beings have innate feelings about the family enterprise as the archetype of pre-industrial life. Could there be an *instinctual* drive to keep business and family inseparable?

Finally, to what extent do professional advisors (of all disciplines) encourage succession planning and warn against "failing" to perpetuate a family business? When this happens, is it because we envy the client's wealth and power, and can't imagine anyone not wanting to be Dwayne Andreas?[1] Or are we merely reflecting what prospective clients want to hear instead of challenging their assumptions?

Consulting Orientation

The Family Firm Institute should make us sign a pledge *not* to make facilitating family business succession our professional mission. Succession can be a failure, when it occurs as a result of developmental failure in a family. Conversely, a thoroughly successful outcome for a family business may be the decision to dispose of it (Le Van, 1998; Tagiuri and Davis, 1982).

The key for consultants is to beware the assumption that something is wrong with people who don't "succeed" at succession—and something right, by definition, with those who do. Frequently, insurance and estate planners bemoan their clients who commission wonderful plans but don't execute them: What's wrong with those people, the advisors wonder, that stops them from doing the presumably successful thing? Could it be that the "best laid plan" is wrong? Could it be that deep down the client knows it isn't good for the family?

As reported in Kaye (1996), a family dynamics (psychology or organizational development) consultant can group family firms according to whether they possess the necessary ingredients for a transition to currently active successors (about a quarter of the author's practice, with whom our "success rate" runs close to 100%), or the ingredients would be present if one or more members can first be liberated from destructive positions and attitudes (about two fifths of this practice, with only about a 33% success rate), or the would-be successors simply aren't capable of working together for a promising transition (about a third of my clients). "Success" in the latter case would mean helping the family take positive steps toward terminating their shared business ownership. By that definition, I am successful with only about 10% of that group (Kaye, 1996). Shouldn't our goal as a profession be to improve that poor success rate for happy landings? How

---

1.   CEO of Archer Daniels Midland, Inc., one of the largest family owned firms in the world. His name was in the news at the time, due to a scandal—KK

should we educate those clients, reframe their goals, prepare them and counsel them?

An approach that I have adopted is to focus on the word *opportunity*. I congratulate parents on the opportunities their success has created for the next generation, get them talking about how far the family has come from humble roots, and then ask the younger members how they feel about those opportunities. They feel appreciative, of course; though they haven't always expressed that to their parents. I emphasize advantages in the broadest sense, including appropriate examples of both external and internal advantages, with the aim of gaining all members' agreement to define success in those terms, regardless who winds up owning the business. Parental success means providing those opportunities at times when their children's lives can best capitalize on them. Inheritor success means making the most of those opportunities, not ruining or being ruined by them.

When substantial wealth is involved, we find it helpful to discuss the major challenges ahead whether they keep the operating business or not (Hamilton, 1992). It is the wealth, not the business, that presents opportunities as well as problems, which these task-oriented entrepreneurs can sink their problem-solving teeth into more readily than they can think about "letting go."

In my experience, the families that do manage to keep their firms successfully over generations are mainly those that *don't have to do so*. Only those whose members have other paths on which they could have succeeded, alternative opportunities they were capable of taking, seem to have talents and experiences that make them likely to thrive in business together. Unfortunately, many families that *cannot* pass their enterprises successfully to the next generation are those that can least afford not to—because their children are ill-equipped for success elsewhere. This means that clients can benefit much more, the earlier they seek counsel or encounter books, articles, forum programs, and so forth.

What about the succession cases? (I give them, rather than ourselves, credit for their virtually inevitable progress through the process.) Notwithstanding the 100% "success rate," they seldom achieve a perfect outcome. As one client said, "Yeah, of course we'll make it, but what will be the quality of our relationship when we're done?" Rarely is it better than it was before. If the dream of being closer and more comfortable with each other, or of being appreciated by a son, daughter, parent, or sibling wasn't realized by 20 years of working together, it isn't going to happen through a succession process. Individuals may come to accept themselves and their families as good enough. Even with such modest goals, though, the quality of family relationships after business transition is a measure of the consultant's success. With clients whose legal/financial transitions are assured, how can we be satisfied with ourselves as consultants unless we also helped them wind up in a good family place?

The role of a family business consultant should not be to increase the number of families whose firms survive into the next generation, but to *narrow* the number to just those whose family businesses enhance their lives. For that group, our role is to help them make a transition that increases the opportunity for all members. For others, it is to help them exchange the business for its worth in new opportunities.

Conclusion

The words *success* and *succession* are still used as synonyms—mistakenly, when family firms are concerned. We decry tax-driven planning, yet we are guilty of a comparable blindness if our avowed mission is succession-driven rather than health-driven. We should be in the business of helping entrepreneurs discover whether their overlapping family and business roles are good for them in the long run. "Is this business healthy for our family? If it cramps our personal growth or hurts our relationships, how can we change that?"

Veteran pilots like to say that a good landing is any landing everybody walks away from; and it's a *great* landing if the plane can be flown again. In family business terms, it is a happy ending when the whole family survives with their capital free to create new opportunities for all, and with appreciation for how thoughtfully and earnestly their business stewards created those opportunities.

References

Hamilton, S. (1992). A second family business—patterns in wealth management. *Family Business Review, 5(2)*, 181-188.

Herbert, James (1989). *Black Male Entrepreneurs and Adult Development*. New York: Praeger.

Kaye, K. (1991). Penetrating the cycle of sustained conflict. *Family Business Review, 4(1)*, 21-44.

Kaye, K. (1992). The kid brother. *Family Business Review, 5(3)*, 237-256.

Kaye, K. (1996). When the family business is a sickness. *Family Business Review, 9(4)*, 347-368.

Le Van, Gerald (1998). *Survival Guide for Business Families*. New York: Routledge.

Tagiuri, R., & Davis, J. (1982) Bivalent attributes of the family firm. Working Paper, Harvard Business School. Reprinted 1996, *Family Business Review, 9(2)*, 199-208.

§

MORE PEOPLE seem to remember the following article than any of the others. Maybe it's because we can all relate to the effect of marriage on parent-child relationships, whether we're in a family business or not.

§

Mate Selection and the Family Business*

An index of a family's success is the caliber of talent it manages to attract and retain through marriage. This fundamental fact in sociology, anthropology, and history has received little attention in the family business field. Parents in Western societies have two windows of opportunity to enhance long-term family success through marriage: first, before their children reach puberty; and later, after they choose spouses for themselves.

1. **THE SON** of an entrepreneurial family, who had low self-esteem and only two years of college, married someone he had known since their childhood religious camp. They cared for and respected each other; it seemed a marriage likely to last. Although she lacked sophistication and talent, his parents, whose litmus test was religious denomination, were pleased.

2. The daughter of an extremely dominant entrepreneur found a husband who did her thinking for her, as her father had. Her new husband accepted a job with the family business, and immediately became inordinately interested in salary, perquisites, and what he called "our" expected inheritance. Her parents were disappointed, wondering why their daughter had made such a poor choice and saddled their business with an ungrateful dependent.

3. A son married a woman whose master's degree in accounting outshone the educational level of everyone in his family. Far from being threatened by her, they were delighted.

4. A daughter with no interest in her family business went to graduate school to study in an esoteric field that her parents considered a dead end. She married and moved with her husband to the opposite end of the country, where their academic jobs eventually brought them a secure though limited income, and great benefits that included subsidized private education for their children and long

*   *Family Business Review, 1999*, Vol. XII, pp. 107-115. Reprinted with permission from the Family Firm Institute, Inc. All rights reserved. The author thanks Dr. Catherine McCarthy and colleagues at the fourth annual retreat on Psychosocial Dynamics of Family Business, for their valuable comments.

vacations. Her father kept hinting that his son-in-law could "make real money" whenever they were ready to move back to Indiana.

This article discusses a frequent, long-standing source of conflict between the generations in wealthy families. In fact, this conflict arises in most middle-class families as well, whether or not they own a business; and it is a universal theme in world literature: Who is a suitable mate for one's child? If it's a society where parents arrange marriages, how can they prevent rebellion like that of Shakespeare's Juliet? In a world where parents are barely consulted, how can they influence their children's matrimonial choices, and how can children marry for *both* love and their parents' approval?

My thesis is that the two generations share a goal, which is rarely made explicit, to build the family's human and intellectual capital. There are consistent mistakes that lead families into conflict over mate selection; but there are also consistent principles that characterize families like the one in my third example, in which both generations feel successful. I think we can define family success in mate selection; and in this paper, I propose that even in our individualistic, anti-authoritarian society, parents have considerable influence on mate selection.

Preserving or dissipating wealth

In a recent speech to stewards of large family fortunes, the CEO of a 5th-generation firm with more than 40 shareholders and beneficiaries referred to "The Four Evils." The evils, he said, by which he meant the enemies of all who would pass wealth to descendants, are inflation, taxation, consumption, and over-procreation. (He assumed that preserving family wealth is desirable.) His audience well knew how those four inescapable factors mathematically erode and dissipate financial capital.

Those four "evils" are only part of the story, as financial capital is only part of it. With the best financial planning in the world, a family's human and intellectual capital can wither, frustrating its progenitors' dreams. And by that I mean *all* the progenitors. Individuals who inherit financial wealth typically trace it back to the success of one couple, encouraging the conceit that the family's identity and heritage derive only from those "founders". Hence the genealogical inverted tree structure. Yet intellectual and human capital flow from all four grandparents and all eight great-grandparents. For someone to fancy herself "a Rockefeller" (for example) gives undue status to a small fraction of her ancestry—based on money, not necessarily brains or character.

Of course, the founders who started with little or no financial capital were using their human resources to create wealth. As the U.S. has proved in the last fifty years, economic growth in a free market society enriches entrepreneurs far more than it does the already wealthy. That fact alone speaks to the significance of human and intellectual capital. The rich get richer, for about one generation. After that, it is the smart, the hard-working, and the dedicated who get richer at the expense of families who are complacent.

Therefore, although parents throughout history have worried about who enters the family through marriage, it is especially significant in a class-permeable society. Mate selection is a fifth evil for financially successful families to worry about—but it can also present opportunity for securing a family's advantages.

Family business success equals increase in children's advantage

Entrepreneurs and investors often measure success and failure in terms of net worth: How much have we increased it? Are we continuing to move up the scale from shirtsleeves to tailored suits, from rice paddy to palace (Hughes, 1997), or are we regressing to the middle class—or worse? (As the CEO speaker suggested, fecundity puts enormous pressures on wealth-building requirements just to stay level, let alone move up the scale.)

A measure of parents' success is the extent to which they create opportunities for their children, enabling the next generation to start their adult lives with an advantage over other young adults in the same society. The true measure of how well parents have done is how much they have *increased* their children's competitive advantages, relative to wherever they themselves started two or three decades earlier.

Successful parents might provide opportunities in the form of a healthy business, a professional degree, investment capital, a strong network of personal connections, or by what the child carries inside, including intelligence, mental health, sound principles, and positive self-esteem. Most of us try to give our children as many competitive advantages as we can, and parents in many cultures actively arrange or restrict marriages in hopes of securing family advancement, or at least preventing a backslide down the slippery socioeconomic slope. We do that because the drive to create advantages for offspring is a biological instinct.

Quantitatively, parental success can be defined as the *value added to next-generation opportunity*. Such a definition embraces those who do not enter the business as well as those who do. It refers to the average opportunity per child across the whole family, including both genders, brilliant children as well as dull ones, regardless of their proclivities and gifts.

Family success has nothing to do with retaining ownership of a business. In fact, entrepreneurially created opportunities take many different forms, most of which are better accessed with cash (for postgraduate tuition, travel, investment, politics, philanthropy, financial independence, etc.) than with the inside track to a job in a parent's company.

The value added to all siblings' head starts in life by their parents' enterprise is a nice theoretical quantification of success, but it is hard to measure in practice. Mate selection, though only a component of the value-adding or-detracting process, has for centuries served as a rough practical index of family success. Probably this is because people have seen that the ability to help children "marry well" distinguishes families who continue to create opportunities from those who ultimately do not.

Open systems

The connection between family business success and marriage is an essential feature of family systems theory.

Entropy is the inevitable breakdown of structure. Nothing defeats entropy, but living systems are remarkably good at resisting it for periods of time ranging from minutes to eons. Because they maintain their structure, complexity, and energy by interacting with their environments, organisms, families, and organizations are called *open* systems, and as such are subject to entropy. All open systems use self-regulatory processes to speed up or slow down, grow larger or downsize, increase or decrease their purchase of materials, stockpile or use up inventories, eliminate more or less waste, ship more or less of their products, all in the service of maintaining the necessary equilibrium for long-term survival of their genes (Dawkins, 1989). If the open system we are talking about is a closely held business, it does those things for long-term survival of the family's identity, values, heritage—the social equivalent of its genes—as well as for the owners' actual DNA.

Consider the defining characteristics of open systems:

- They import energy (find and exploit external resources).

- They eliminate waste products.

- They create information (organization, as opposed to randomness).

- They perpetuate themselves.

- If they can, they grow; but if growth endangers their perpetuation, they downsize.

- If they become *closed* systems (shut off from external resources or from ways of shedding material they cannot use), they die.

In short, the key to all open systems is finding, exploiting, and organizing *external* resources. That is why a system like a family-owned business, in which one of the goals is to increase the opportunity advantages of its owners' children, must reach out beyond its boundaries for educational and technological resources to put at the service of the family members. For example, their business must employ the most talented non-family members they can recruit. Otherwise, it is a closed, or doomed, system.

Exogamous tribes

The point about non-family executives has been made before. But there are two ways a family manages to attract outside talent, through the recruitment of non-family executives to run its enterprises and through marriage. If both are accomplished together, either because someone enters the family through marriage who turns out to be a valuable business recruit or because a great executive turns up in the business and later marries into the family, so much the better. Of the two kinds of search, executive and marital, the latter consumes much more personal attention, for good reasons—and it deserves our professional attention as well.

In marriage choices, as in executive recruitment, success requires what anthropologists call *exogamy* (Greek roots meaning *out-marrying*): reaching beyond the tribe for new genetic, cultural, or technological resources. In business terms, exogamy means filling a position through an outside search, acquiring intellectual, social, and managerial assets for the family through marriage—not settling for the boy or girl next door. The marriages children make can produce enormous gains for a business family, not only in financial capital, but also in emotional and intellectual capital: in education, experience, and technological resources. Or their marriages can drag the family backward. Marriages can be a means of recruiting great business managers into a family, or a harbinger of business suicide. But they are important, even when neither spouse works in the business, because every marriage choice has profound implications for the gene pool and for the psychological health of the following generation.

Of course, openness to new kinds of people isn't the first instinct of a parent or of a business owner, who are more likely to look within their own social group. Openness is risky. Just as recruiting talented managers, or a CEO, or board members requires a thoughtful balance between the need for new blood and the importance of a good fit with elements of the corporate culture that are working well, so too does the search for a mate involve balancing novelty with comfort. Spouses should share a language, fundamental values, and a set of expectations about roles and mutual reliance. But they also need to surprise, delight, and challenge each other.

For parents, there is an issue of trust every time children marry outside the tribe. We trust others in proportion to how well we think we know them. When a potential son-or daughter-in-law's background is very different from our own, trust may take a little longer to establish. It is human to be more comfortable, initially, with someone who has all the right credentials on paper, someone who plays golf or tennis, belongs to the right church or synagogue, attended the right schools, and has the right season tickets. However, such trust can be misplaced. Someone with the right credentials can turn out to be a wastrel or a scoundrel, or simply an airhead.

Should matchmaking be a new family business consulting specialty?

When I work with a family whose younger generation has already married, I often feel that those decisions and actions already taken will have greater effect on their fortunes than anything with which I can help. How the next generation of parents raise their children is more significant for their long-term chances of preserving family wealth than any business decisions they make.

With young adults who are still single, the kind of people they are likely to marry was probably determined years ago. Their range of marriage opportunities and the choices they will make within that range were shaped in childhood and adolescence.

Although I don't plan to add a matchmaking page to my website, I sometimes offer a word of counsel on this subject to the older or younger generations:

Advice to Parents: The lesson from happy families—and it is consistent with everything we know about developmental psychology—is that our only chance to influence our children's choice of mate successfully is by preparing them early to make good choices when the time comes. Recognizing that our children are going to choose for themselves (for better or worse), we need to begin doing the things listed in Table 1 when our children are young. If the list falls into three pairs of do's and don'ts, it is because the parental art is a balancing act.

Your own marriage is the best model your children will have as they envision what it would be like to marry a particular individual. No marriage is perfect, so be sure they know what the strengths of your marriage are, or were. (They probably have a fine sense of its weak points.)

Table 1. How to maximize descendants' competitive advantages: advice to parents of young children and adolescents

Raise their sights

♦ Develop each child's fullest potential in the fields of his or her strength, even if those have nothing to do with the family business. The more accomplished they are, the more talented, accomplished, and healthy will be the people they attract as mates.

♦ At the same time, build self-esteem that is independent of prizes and external accolades. (Individuals who feel intrinsically good about themselves will be attractive to, and attracted to, more talented people as mates.)

Prime the pump

♦ Create economic opportunities through the business or through prudent wealth management, and make children aware that doors will thereby open for them.

♦ On the other hand, beware of creating false entitlement, the attitude that "worth" is the same as "net worth," or that money buys happiness.

Remove blinders

♦ Encourage the choice of a mate based on diverse qualities, rather than narrow prejudices.

♦ At the same time, frankly discourage "marrying down." While it is stupid to label a marriage prospect unworthy because he or she comes from a family with no money or with a different ethnic background, other criteria are meaningful. If your teenager is dating a boy or girl who seems less than bright, who is lazy, irresponsible, or mistreats your child, it would be a disservice to withhold that observation. You should express your concern. (Above all, children must be taught not to marry anyone under the delusion that the person will change.)

Unfortunately, most parents wait until their son or daughter has fallen in love with someone, and then they either breathe a sigh of relief or try to pose objections: She is not Jewish, or he is not Catholic, or not Italian, or not from "a good family." That is a sure formula for family conflict. If they break up, your child may blame you. If they marry anyway, your new in-law comes into the family as an opponent. Therefore, by early adulthood or even adolescence, the more directly you attempt to influence a child's marriage choices, the more spectacularly you will fail. The best practice is to accept the fact that there is no way to interfere with a child's poor marriage choice without making the situation worse.

After accepting a new family member, there are many things you can do to bring out the best in that person. The chief point, indicated throughout Table 2, is to concentrate on strengths. How can family resources be used to enhance the gifts he or she brings, from experience as well as from nature? What can you do to support the young couple's sense of full responsibility for the family's future? And if you do have serious reservations about the individual—for example, stupidity, laziness, addiction, or irresponsibility—all you can do is avoid feeding the problem: Do not protect the in-law from accountability. However, any active judgmental position is unlikely to help and very likely to undermine your own goals.

And remember, you do not have to employ him or her. The temptation and external pressure to do so may be greater, the less productively employable the individual is; but the long-term consequences of yielding to that temptation warrant careful thought, case by case.

Finally, prenuptial agreements are infinitely less effective than having trained your child to choose a mate wisely. At best, a prenuptial contract protects financial capital. It takes great sensitivity to do the latter without damaging the human capital.

Advice to Young People: Before committing yourself to marriage—if you intend to produce children—ask whether this is the person you would want raising them in case you were to die before they were grown.

Don't marry anyone to spite your parents, or just because he or she contrasts with them. With all their faults, don't your parents possess some qualities that you would need in a spouse?

Most importantly, understand the valid reasons for their concern about who you bring into the family. Even if you discount their opinions about your happiness and well-being, consider their thinking about the three kinds of family wealth. Their criteria may be crazy, and their methods repulsive, and their timing ten or twenty years too late—but they are correct in thinking that this decision has enormous ramifications for the continued building (or rapid squandering) of everything for which they have worked.

Table 2. How to maximize descendants' competitive advantages: advice to parents-in-law

---

Work with the strengths

  • What positive traits (education, intelligence, moral character, creativity, artistic talent, energy, social network, etc.) does your new daughter- or son-in-law offer the family?
  • Which family resources can be used, without making him or her uncomfortable, to leverage those strengths as much as possible? (E.g, tuition to pursue more education, or a responsibility in the family or the business that can provide a showcase, training, exposure to broader horizons, etc.)

Don't fuel a problem

  • If we have reservations about the habits and expectations this individual came to us with, is there anything we should stop doing, that has been maintaining or exacerbating those counter-cultural norms or destructive behaviors?
  • *Never ask* "How can we (or our son/daughter) fix the problem?"—because that usually makes it worse.

Full membership

  • Are we treating this individual as a full-fledged family member?   This does not necessarily mean equal salary, or inheritance; it does mean equal opportunity to use family resources in ways that build human, intellectual, and financial capital for future generations.

Advice to Consultants: The examples in the opening section of this article come from the author's own practice. The first young man married down, in that his wife didn't seem to have the intelligence (of any kind) to hold her own with his family. She lacked sophistication, ambition, and talent. Fortunately, his parents were so pleased with the young couple's religious fealty that they failed to realize their good daughter-in-law represented a potentially significant hindrance to their family's continued upward mobility. (No, I didn't tell them. I do recognize that my definition of long-term family success—enhancement of opportunity—ignores such trivialities as love and happiness. All four of the couples in my examples married for love, and are happy together.)

In the second example, the parents wondered why their daughter saddled both herself and their business with an ungrateful dependent. They didn't see that both of those problems were of their own making. They should have given her more respect for herself, of course, and even after she married the mooch, they didn't have to give him a job for which he was unqualified and a salary he didn't earn. It *is* the consultant's job to raise that issue.

In the third example, the family improved itself through marriage. The young man's parents described their accountant daughter-in-law as a "prize," regardless of whether she worked in the business or (as happened) chose to stay at home while her children were young.

In example 4, neither the daughter nor her husband worked in the business. Nonetheless, her exogamous marriage is an index of the family business's success. Why? Because it was the income from that business that gave her the opportunity to pursue a satisfying career, and marry someone with his own satisfying career. Philosophy had not been a vocational option for either of her parents. Furthermore, when, in a couple of decades, the daughter's children become beneficiaries of the generation-skipping trusts her parents created, they are likely to be well equipped both intellectually and emotionally to manage that substantial wealth sensibly.

If, as outside consultants, we share this perspective about the importance of children's education, self-esteem, values, and attracting new blood, should we and can we sell that perspective to our clients? I think we can, somewhat, sometimes.

In the United States, our present-day culture increases the challenge for advisors. Parents play such limited roles in mate selection; why do I even bring up the subject? We don't live in a world of arranged marriages. However, parents do inculcate snobbery and prejudices in their children, and they do discourage contact with people they assume are inferiors. A sociobiologist might say that such prejudices serve the same function in narrowing a child's search criteria as they would in an arranged marriage culture.

The notion of "marrying up" or "marrying down" may sound like something out of a nineteenth-century novel—worrying about what society will say—but that is absolutely not what I mean. Our definition of family success refers to actual competitive advantage, *avoiding* the prejudicial errors of one's community. Parents' initial assessment of the candidate's human capital is often based on the wrong criteria: inadequate litmus tests such as race, religion, and class.

Nor am I referring to the prospective mate's family's money. Of course, a family may acquire financial capital through marriage; but that is rarely as significant as what it acquires or fails to acquire in human capital.

Perhaps our most constructive role is to challenge members of both generations to think about the actual qualities of individuals who may be candidates for joining the family, from wherever they come. And we can push parents to see how their long-term goals for their families depend on the quality of relationships they build with sons-and daughters-in-law.

Among business-owning families, we encounter all four types of "in-law" situations exemplified above: those that enhance the family in some way (3 and 4) and those that do not (1 and 2); and in either case, parents who realize the fact (2 and 3) and those who do not (1 and 4). Would it be useful for a consultant to advise an entrepreneur whose business seems to be declining and whose sons and daughters are models of mediocrity, "Try to get your kids to marry people more capable and self-confident than themselves?" Obviously not—it would be too late. The time for parents to receive the advice in Table 1 would have been many years before they engaged us as advisors.

Nor would we say to the client described in the first example, "You're foolish to feel so complacent about your son's marriage. Your daughter-in-law may be easy for you to relate to because she shares so many of your convictions, but she brings nothing to your family other than a below-average IQ, a lack of imagination, spinelessness (which you like, as she doesn't challenge you), and dull-witted grandchildren."

On the other hand, what about the daughter and son-in-law described in the last example? Her parents appreciated my pointing out that their business success had allowed her to enjoy an academic life without worrying about accumulating wealth.

Finally, in example 2, the parents are justifiably concerned about the impact of their son-in-law on both the business and the family. They may need the consultant's help in building appropriate safeguards into the governance structure and succession processes, as well as assertiveness about such touchy matters as prenuptial agreements and restrictive trusts.

A needed dissertation

What we are discussing is no less than a theory about mate selection and successful families. It raises the possibility of observing one of the ways a family business system succeeds or fails to use external resources for its own advantage. If we are right in calling our client families "systems," we should be able to make some long-term predictions about their viability. Of course, we won't confuse family success with keeping the business in the family (Kaye, 1996).

I would suggest that anyone who hopes to assess the strength of a family enterprise, or of any fortunate family, might better derive an index of success from the quality of people who marry members of that family than from any complex and elusive set of measures on the members themselves.

How could this theory be tested? Find fifty families whose fortunes over a couple of generations clearly moved in the positive direction. Compare them with fifty families whose fortunes declined relative to the society as a whole. If I am right in postulating mate selection as an index of the families' success, then the average educational level, occupational index, or both, of spouses who married into those families during the two previous generations will differ significantly between the upwardly and downwardly mobile samples.

Hughes (1997) advocates measuring a family's human and intellectual capital, and tracking it over time. I'm saying that such an assessment would need to include the family members who enter by attachment, not only by birth, and that the relative talents of those people alone might prove a good index of the whole family's success.

Even if some data could be found to test this hypothesis and the results supported the theory, processes of cause and effect would still remain to be studied. My theory is that the long-term progress of family fortunes (opportunity advantages for descendants, relative to their cohorts) is the outcome of behavior listed in Table 1. The importance of self-esteem in child development suggests that those recommendations are the best way to help one's children attract the most promising family wealth enhancers.

Conclusion

Research in evolutionary biology confirms Darwin's observation that diversity is a key to adaptation (Weiner, 1994). It follows that too little diversity and too much mediocrity in marriage partners pose long-term threats to family systems' competitive advantages.

We do our clients a disservice if we facilitate their succession and estate planning, focussing on the problem of preserving their financial capital, without equal or greater emphasis on their human and intellectual capital. As Jay Hughes puts it,

> Financial capital alone cannot provide long-term wealth preservation. What a family's financial capital can provide is a powerful tool to promote the growth of its human and intellectual capital. After all, without human capital there are no family assets; there is no family! Without intellectual capital, under-educated family members with all the money in the world will not make enough good decisions over a long period of time to outnumber their bad decisions. Successful long-term wealth preservation lies in understanding that it is the growth of a family's human and intellectual capital that determines its success, and that the growth of its financial capital provides a powerful tool to achieve this success. (Hughes, 1997)

Of the ways parents can influence all three kinds of capital, their ability to influence children's mate selection is among the least direct. At best it happens through indirect influence (role modeling, inculcating values, self-esteem) and only over the whole course of childhood, adolescence, and early adulthood. Yet the effect of those marriage choices on subsequent generations' opportunities is greater than any of those factors a parent can influence more directly. It may be as great as all the direct factors combined.

As for parents whose children have chosen unwisely, the best advice is to ask not what you can do to weaken the relationship, but whether a more strategic and judicious use of family resources can leverage that individual's strengths while avoiding the perpetuation of problems.

References

Dawkins, Richard, *The Selfish Gene*. Oxford: Oxford University Press, 1989.

Hughes, Jay, *Family Wealth: Keeping It in the Family*. NY: James E. Hughes, Jr., 1997.

Kaye, Kenneth, When the family business is a sickness. *Family Business Review*, 1996, *IX* (4), 347-368.

Weiner, Jonathan. *The Beak of the Finch*. NY: Knopf, 1994.

§

MANY THEMES in all the foregoing articles come together in this one, written with Sara Hamilton, about working with third-, fourth-, or fifth-generation families of substantial inherited wealth. In an article aimed at trust and estate attorneys (Hamilton & Kaye, 2003), we quoted F. Scott Fitzgerald's remark, "The very rich are different from you and me," and Ernest Hemingway's famous rejoinder: "Yes, they have more money."

We added, "They also have more money managers, trustees, and advisors. For great wealth always entails the delegation of responsibilities and authority. Death forces the ultimate delegation. And every estate plan represents a set of decisions about what should be entrusted to whom, for what purpose."

This article addresses the dynamics of the whole system, including inheritors, trustees, contingent beneficiaries, spouses and minor children, their full-time professional staffs, and assorted outside advisors.

§

The Role of Trust in Consulting to Financial Families*

Kenneth Kaye, Sara Hamilton

Trust is not only crucial to success among the owners of substantial wealth, it is also the sine qua non for successful teamwork among professionals who work with them. There can be dangers, however, in too much trust and too little healthy confrontation, just as there are in mistrust and chronic conflict.

ACONSULTING ASSIGNMENT becomes more complex as there are more family branches; as those branches are tied together in more business relationships; as more corporations, partnerships, and trusts own their assets; as they do business in more states and foreign countries; as they have more advisors involved; and as transition events approach (a leader retiring, a matriarch passing away, a trust terminating, a business being sold, etc.). Complicating factors can also include publicly traded stock, a family's prominence, a tragedy or a scandal, and of course, the whole gamut of addictions and other mental health issues.

Although much of this article will apply to all family business consulting, financial families are defined as those that are complex in all or most of the ways mentioned above.

The authors are, respectively, a psychologist specializing in conflict resolution and successor development in family firms of all sizes, and the founder/CEO of Family Office Exchange, an organization that assists owners of substantial wealth with multi-generational family office and wealth management. Co-consulting to such cases has sharpened our focus on some problems about trust. Here we refer

* *Family Business Review*, 2004, Vol. XVII, pp. 151-163. Reprinted with permission from the Family Firm Institute, Inc. All rights reserved. Co-author Sara Hamilton is Founder and CEO of Family Office Exchange, Inc., www.foxexchange.com. The authors thank Marta Vago for helpful comments on a draft of the manuscript.

not to the legal entity, *a trust* (a property interest held by one person for the benefit of another), but to the vital aspect of all human relationships, *trust* (reliance on another's character, ability, strength, or truthfulness).

Family Office Exchange, Inc., has collected data on more than 2000 families owning between $100 million and several billion in assets. Financial families highlight the roles of trust, especially with regard to three constant challenges of consulting work:

- *Constant Challenge #1:* devote careful attention to the working alliance between consultants and clients;

- *Constant Challenge #2:* always build processes that will accommodate change, rather than permanent structures the clients will have to live within;

- *Constant Challenge #3:* bring together a multidisciplinary consulting team, and manage relationships among its members as well as the family's long-term advisors and key employees. Different disciplines will be required in different cases, but they will normally include at least one "content" person who concentrates on the legal entities, forms of governance or management, and knowledge of applicable best practices for the given type of business; while at least one "process person" is primarily tuned to the interactions, human development, and unconscious group dynamics. Both types must have some training in, and be alert to the other's perspective.

The above three challenging aspects of consultation are today widely accepted in the literature and practice (Swartz, 1989; Hilburt-Davis & Senturia, 1995; Bork, Jaffe, Lane, Dashew, & Heisler, 1995; Davidow & Narva, 2001). This article discusses them in connection with trust among family members, among outsiders, and between the two groups.

There is a growing literature on the role of trust within business families (Powell, 1987; Bradach & Eccles, 1989; Kaye, 1995; LaChapelle & Barnes, 1998; Lansberg, 1999; Steier, 2001; Hamilton & Kaye, 2003). There is also literature on trust in the process of advising these families (Alderfer, 1988; Whiteside & Brown, 1991; Kaye, 1994). We argue that managing trust is the *sine qua non* when working with all sizes of family firms.

The Trust Catalyst

A central concept throughout this discussion is that of the *trust catalyst*. LaChapelle & Barnes (1998) pointed out that amid the frustrations, anxieties, and disharmony that can hamper the work of a business family, often one person helps create higher trust. The same person maintains that role for years, even decades. It could be the wife and mother of an owner and his children. It could be a high-status friend of the parents, respected by the younger generation without the ambivalence of a parent/child relationship. (In *The Sopranos*, Hesh Rabkin, old friend of Tony Soprano's father, is the guy everyone wants at the table if they have to arrange a "sit-down".) A trust catalyst may be an uncle, an in-law, an attorney or other long-term advisor. In multi-branch families, it can be one of the CEO's siblings or cousins, or even a member of the successor generation. In many businesses, a non-family president, CFO, or head of Human Resources provides a bridge of trust between the generations.

LaChapelle and Barnes used the word *catalyst* because these members inspire other family members and business partners to trust each other. Family members basically want to do so, but past experiences have put them on guard. Trust catalysts serve as reminders of the family "glue". They seem to put a damper on conflict, often by little more than being good listeners and remaining calm. LaChapelle and Barnes give examples of successful transitions aided by the presence of a trust catalyst in the family business. They contrast those with some examples of chronic conflicts when no one fills that role.

Clearly, in interviewing a family and its key employees, consultants should look for the existence of one or more trust catalysts. However, one should not assume that their effect is always salutary. We will revisit the concept of the trust catalyst as we explore each of the three constant challenges in family consultations.

Constant Challenge #1: Awareness of the Alliance

The greatest determiner of successful change in a family business is the consultants' ability to maintain a working alliance with leaders in the client system—and to keep moving the engagement forward step by step (Vago, 2003). Clinical psychologists call it the "therapeutic alliance." This is a more consistent factor in success than the consultants' stores of knowledge (management, law, family systems theory, best practices in human resources or in wealth management or in family office administration). The alliance affects the success of a consultation more than how "dysfunctional" the system appears to be, how profitable the business is, or the size of the assets at stake. First and foremost, we have to engage with the family business system—in fact, become temporarily part of it—so we ourselves can exercise leadership within it. To put this another way, if the family doesn't have a trust catalyst already, we need to perform that role, for awhile; and if they do, we need to be another one.

When clients make progress by achieving a stated objective—for example, adopt a mission statement or a set of by-laws, resolve a family member's desire to take his equity out of the business, agree on new roles, hire a new CEO, or establish a family office—the consultant keeps the engine running and ready to depart as soon as the passengers are ready for the next stage of their journey. But even when the process stalls, or regresses a step or two, the alliance enables consultants to reassure the clients, alleviate anxieties, resolve conflicts, and get the train back on the track.

If the consultants are wise and skillful and their styles and values are compatible with those of the client family, then the clients will have made a valuable investment in the consultants' learning about the family members, their business challenges, and their long-term needs. The consultants have developed rapport and learned how to communicate differently with individual family members. The clients may have asked for help with a single event, but this was a step in a long process with which they'll need help, from various professionals, over the years. Frankly, they need to be shown what they're really in the midst of. They usually don't know what questions to ask. They know what hurts, but not why. They don't know which problems will lessen with time, and which will get worse if untreated. If this makes consulting sound like a sales job, so it is. (The first author prefers to see himself as Yoda in *Star Wars*.)

Conversely, if consultants lose an engagement because the clients blame them for a painful experience that didn't achieve its objective, *or* it achieves an objective without raising awareness about the big picture, then not only have the consultants lost future business, but the clients have wasted the time and money they invested in the consultants' learning about them.

Family business consultants reveal how important the personal alliance is when we present a case to colleagues at a conference or workshop. We invariably tell the story as a sequence of interpersonal moments. If we're presenting a fairly successful consultation, we may describe a "stuck" phase where their resistance to change had us temporarily stymied, and then we'll say, "That's when cousin Bob called me" (indicating a key person on the genogram).

In those same presentations, we consultants often explain our failures by pointing to key members on the chart with whom we were unable to form a constructive personal relationship. For example, one of the authors was two years into an engagement with a family. This family suffered from a longstanding rift between the CEO (who was also the sole active trustee of a dynasty trust) and his wife, on one side, versus the rest of the family. When the wife made a hurtful remark about another family member in our meeting, the author's attempt at neutral intervention alienated her. A few months later he resigned, since he had lost the trust of a powerful, besieged branch of the family. He had been unable to make the case for better tolerance because of his own failure to establish a good enough alliance with both sides.

That failure was particularly instructive because the client system did have a trust catalyst. The family office's outside attorney was an expert on their problematic content area—the trusts and holding companies they inherited—but was also sensitive to the emotional upheaval into which their father's death had thrust them. This trust catalyst, in fact, was the one who had brought the author in as family process consultant. But a good alliance between the embedded trust catalyst and the outside consultant wasn't enough. The author had failed to become, himself, a trust catalyst for the family.

Such experiences taught us that our consulting team has to become a temporary member of what Peter Davis called the "sentient system":

> A subsystem [of the whole family business] is the sentient system that has the family at its core and is made of individuals bound by strong emotional and loyalty bonds. The sentient system will generally include nonfamily members who are "drawn into" and become subject to the basic organizing rules of the family" (1983, p. 51).

Constant Challenge #2: Always build processes—and trust is one of them

Creating a process that can accommodate change is much more important than any structure the founder and advisors might devise. Each generation must be prepared for responsibilities their parents can't foresee. The ship is moving. That is why the estate plan should be understood to be as much process as structure. The process must accommodate the development of leadership in the next generation, just as it must accommodate the beneficiaries' changing needs and circumstances. In each generation, the trustees and governing council of a family face a new set of challenges for succession to the next generation. Will the family be able to work together on how to reallocate assets after the sale of a business? How will they handle the evolving administration of a family office, foundation, or trusts? In addition to the functions of those who serve on the Board, processes for the whole family include continually improving communications, resolving conflicts, reaffirming purpose, developing human capital, and perhaps most important of all, continually reassessing how well the trustees and advisors are fulfilling their roles (Hughes, 1997).

Does the importance of processes mean the "process" consultant is the team's leader? No. In fact, he or she may observe from the sidelines much of the time while the "content" consultants educate and stimulate the group. The content expert will be equally concerned that what the clients are building is a set of processes to accommodate change.

We try to teach our clients, when they have problems of mistrust (as all people do), that trust is not black and white. It, too, is a process (Barnes, 1981; Lansberg, 1999; Hamilton & Kaye, 2003). The decision to entrust responsibility to someone is not a binary decision—to do so or not. The question *in whom* to place trust is inseparable from *how much* trust to place, and *in what areas* of responsibility.

In talking with clients, we have found it sufficient to distinguish among three types of trust: ability, honesty, and motives. Is the person competent in this role? Does she tell the truth? Does he work for the whole family's benefit, not merely his own? If one of those kinds of trust is lost, but at least one of the others exists (for example, John doubts Jane's competence but trusts her motives), it may be possible to rebuild the needed trust (Kaye, 1995). Unfortunately, as we all know from our own lives, the destruction of trust can be swift and terrible; its reconstruction slow and exhausting.

The way to build trust is to test it first by entrusting the person with small matters, then bigger ones as he or she proves to have been reliable. The responsibilities of ownership are entrusted in that same way, building from smaller ones (does her public behavior do credit to our name?) to the privilege of participating in meetings, then having a vote, then chairing committees, and so forth.

Two paradigmatic forms of economic organization are "hierarchy" and "market", but there is a literature on other, hybrid forms all along the continuum between them (Powell, 1987; Bradach & Eccles, 1989). Trust determines where an organization fits on that continuum. Steier points out that as a firm evolves through the generations, "in some cases, what was once a very resilient trust is replaced by an atmosphere of fragile trust or even distrust and an important source of strategic advantage is lost" (p. 353). To some extent, this is inevitable in the most harmonious family. The business needs more controls as it grows beyond the day-to-day scope of its family owners. *Any* group of owners will need to reinvest in trust and trust-building activities, over time.

When too little trust leads to too much trust

Too little trust can quickly become a vicious circle. People who mistrust others are very likely to become less trustworthy themselves, as they defensively withhold information and renege on promises. A whole culture of distrust is born, taking hold like cancer, making succession impossible.

On the other hand, a family business can suffer from *too much trust*, as easily as too little. It happens when the sheer amount of learning and work required to exercise responsibilities of ownership tempt members to delegate some tasks that must not be delegated. They don't want to squander their wealth, but they expect it to make their lives easier, not harder.

Owners should never delegate goal-setting, oversight, measuring success and holding the leaders accountable. Nor should owners let anyone else decide how much and how long the assets will be held collectively for the benefit of future generations, or how involved family members will be in managing the wealth process. Yet they do. Ironically, in our experience with financial families, after a founder places *too little* trust in the next generation, they tend to place *too much* trust in one leader, or in outsiders.

Consider the psychological differences between entrepreneur and successors. Staying in control has paid off well for the former. As risk-takers with capital, entrepreneurs trust their own instincts but not those of others. They often guard control and have difficulty trusting even their best employees, let alone their children. And perhaps because they know so well the narrow margin between success and defeat, they distrust their children's ability to make successes of themselves. Many don't seem to want them to succeed (McCollom, 1992). Therefore they tend to favor complex structures, which their children don't understand and don't want to manage.

What happens when the wealth passes from the founder to the second generation? Most sibling groups are more risk averse than their parents were, having been taught to avoid risk and preserve the assets they were so fortunate to inherit. They are more concerned about not losing it than with building more for future generations. So they seek to simplify complex, highly leveraged assets. And they often retain overly-concentrated stock positions, especially in their legacy company. But they have little or no experience with the financial, tax and legal issues, such as the risk/reward tradeoffs surrounding an undiversified asset. The financial services industry makes it difficult for owners to learn what they need to know about the process, as most firms still view client education only as a marketing tool rather than a core business.

Nor are they prepared for governance processes. The inheritors' job is, in some ways, more difficult than the one the founder was doing. They will have to make decisions as a group. They won't have the autocrat's luxury of being able to ignore unappealing suggestions (Lansberg, 1999). Having watched a patriarch operate with sole authority for 30 to 40 years, brothers and sisters and cousins have had no role models for collective ownership.

The next step is almost inevitable. The structures are so complicated—extending, not infrequently, to dozens of partially interlocking partnerships, each with different assets and obligations—that the inheritors have to find sophisticated advisors, and delegate major aspects of financial oversight to others.

Those outsiders, respected for their knowledge and appreciated for relieving anxiety, are well situated to become trust catalysts. An outsider may arrive in this position through actual competence, good intentions, and the well-earned trust of family members. However, it is easy for families to entrust too much to one person. The successors may delegate too much authority to a single family member, business officer, or outside professional. They allow him or her to wear too many hats (for example, attorney, trustee, and director; or CEO of a business and trustee of a foundation that is a major shareholder), with insufficient checks and balances. They may thus create an interest that conflicts with those of the family.

In our experience, when an outsider falls into this position, it usually happens through good intentions and the owners' desire to hold on to trusted relationships. When a business is sold, for example, they want to retain the trusted CFO, so they entrust the family office to him without considering experienced candidates. Yet the skills that made him a wonderful CFO in the entrepreneurial business may be exactly wrong for wealth managing and trust administering. The blind lead the blind into new territory.

In some cases, over-trusting of an outsider occurs for a different reason, which we call the *founder's inverse bias*: "No one in the family can be as smart as Grandfather was. Let's not consider any of our own for such important responsibilities." (Of course, there is another group of families who will *only* trust a family member, and a third group who never commit themselves to trusting anyone at all, for long.)

Financial families vastly underinvest in financial education and in training for leadership roles that owners themselves should fill. Family Office Exchange members spend an average of about $20,000 per family per year, less than one hundredth of one per cent of their assets!

Finally, overtrusting either an outsider or a family member can occur as a result of conflict avoidance. They may be chosen by default. When people sense that they are in over their heads, but are not sure what's wrong, one normal human response is to deny the complexity, to feel greater certitude or false confidence, suppressing unspoken doubts and plunging ahead into the darkness. The family may avoid discussing doubts about one another's competence. They may never have acknowledged those doubts, even privately, so they resolve the question quickly at the first sign of a possible fight.

This problem of trusting by default is doubly dangerous when the recipient is a family member, who in many cases may not have earned any confidence at all in his or her abilities. An outsider probably had to prove something, but with an insider the family may arrive at a flimsy consensus, either a decision to divvy up responsibilities or to delegate them to the member who most wants them. At best, he or she has established credibility in one area, which doesn't transfer to the responsibilities being conferred. Trust is granted, in other words, not having been earned. This postpones and ultimately worsens conflict.

Thus the conflict-avoiding benefits of a trust catalyst carry risks, equally so whether it is an outsider or a family member. The egregious cases, in which such people deliberately cheat their employers or beneficiaries, are few. We have known occasional misappropriations of funds. But there is another, more prevalent kind of damage from relying on too few family members: The others sit back, so to speak, and withdraw their human capital from governance. They're in denial about how much owners and beneficiaries need to know, and to control, if they hope to survive as a wealthy family. When only one or a few family members pay attention to business or wealth matters, their siblings and cousins often forfeit any means of reviewing them and setting their compensation. Nor do they assess trustees' and advisors' performance.

In short, a family can have too little conflict as well as too much. Family harmony can be a trap. We call this kind of consensus "flimsy" because it will fall apart, not having been built on a working foundation. What is needed is a formal process of continual evaluation to guard against the natural human tendency to avoid raising uncomfortable doubts. As Ronald Reagan famously advised, "trust but verify."

Another safety mechanism is the rule that all family business agreements should incorporate exit strategies. We emphasize with our clients that every joint endeavor they enter into, whether a business corporation, investment partnership, family office, or private trust company, must be voluntary in the sense that no individual dissenting partner is trapped in the relationship. One can choose to go along with the majority, but no one should be compelled to participate either by the legal structures or by family pressure. Such compulsion would sooner or later destroy their family bonds, without which their financial partnerships are doomed.

A disaffected member who believes his own interests conflict with the group's should not have to attack or sabotage the shared business. Again, formal procedures make it possible to raise such questions in normal constructive discourse rather than destructively, in helpless rage.

Our data on Family Office Exchange financial families indicate that about 60% of their assets are held in trusts. One reason so many beneficiaries of trusts are dissatisfied is the "arranged marriage" nature of the structure. Rare is the estate planner who cautions grantors that creating a trust will make its beneficiaries permanent bedfellows (McCollom, 1992).

During a consulting engagement, the presence of the multidisciplinary team reduces the risk of premature agreement. One advisor may be so convinced that the proposed agreement is in everyone's interest that he misses the lack of conviction with which they are agreeing to it. But the second or third set of eyes and ears, tuned at that time to the process more than the content, can interrupt and ask those who seem to be withholding their doubts to put them on the table.

Constant Challenge #3: The multidisciplinary team

The authors we cited in the introductory section of this article, among others, have discussed the necessity of working either as a practiced partnership of professionals from several disciplines, or a well-coordinated ad hoc group of advisors who find themselves involved with the same family (Barber, Hilburt-Davis, McKillip, Swartz, & Wofford, 2002). Increasingly, especially with financial families, a team of two or three consulting partners will need to coordinate with a number of long-time advisors as well as the family leaders.

Unpredictable issues will surface in the course of such engagements, requiring the professional team to function flexibly and creatively, and to communicate efficiently among themselves. All of which means that *trust is as vital in the consultant subsystem as it is in the sentient subsystem of the family business.* If trust is vital, the consultants and advisors themselves are likely to need at least one trust catalyst just to moderate their own mutual apprehensions, professional differences and assertive personalities. The lead liaison with the family is probably in the best position to be a trust catalyst for both team and clients. Individual clients will not have time, opportunity, or inclination to form a working alliance with each individual advisor. But if most of the client family members, and especially their own trust catalysts, get comfortable with at least the trust catalyst on the consulting team, the engagement can work productively.

The number of people in a family makes a huge difference in how well consultants can retain their trust. Compare two of our clients with approximately the same collective net worth: slightly over $2 billion. One has nine members, including spouses and children. The other has more than 100, 76 of whom we met.

The Doe family (not their real name) are third generation wealth creators. They grew up in one branch of a very wealthy family, but through separation of assets and their own success they now control a larger, sibling-owned portfolio of businesses. They are a sister and two brothers, in early middle age. This client relationship has evolved over seven years. It began with conflict resolution by one of us, and guidance by the other in helping them hire a family office CEO with strengths appropriate to the transitions they were facing. We continued with close involvement with the new CEO, as well as their business CEO and investment managers. Gradually taking a back seat, our relationship now is primarily information providing. The first author, the therapist member of our team, has found and introduced leading child development and education professionals who provide diagnostic testing, therapy, or schools consultation. Although he still facilitates two family meetings a year, his presence there is that of a trusted resource who knows the history and personalities, rather than a therapist concerned with conflicts or crises. The second author, our family office expert, has direct contact only with their office CEO.

Discussion with many of our colleagues—family process and content experts alike—indicates that this is the norm. One person maintains a long-term advisory relationship, facilitating the clients' trust in a succession of other resources, as needed.

With a larger group, however, it has been our experience that this sort of long-term leadership becomes exponentially more difficult to sustain. This makes sense mathematically: Trust is bound to be attenuated as a family grows branches. Although conflict may not reach the intensity that it does in a nuclear family, the family members know each other less well, and will know the consultants less well. There will be little opportunity to detect and repair those inevitable tears in the fabric of the client-consultant alliance. Every additional family member increases the likelihood that a consultant will fail to maintain someone's trust. Every additional collaborator in the consultation does so as well.

Furthermore, sheer numbers hold back what can be accomplished over any period of time. We planned and facilitated two days of a three-day family retreat for 76 members of the Ray family (51 adults, compared with the Doe family's five). The meeting was exciting, and most participants rated it very worthwhile. One technique we used was to exaggerate the differences in our perspectives, family relationships *versus* returns on financial capital, so as to model our ability to disagree yet actively listen to one another and enjoy our working relationship.

They were a conflict-averse family, by nature and tradition, so we engaged in some respectful debate in front of them (Swartz, 1989). Another technique was to break them out into constituency groups that had never before expressed distinct positions; for example, all the in-laws in one room, all the 18 to 30 year olds (some of whom barely knew one another) in another room. In each case, a new perspective emerged, which they reported to the whole family for the first time. This exercise broke up what our interviewees had described as entrenched factions.

Those two days led them to add members to existing committees, form at least one new committee, and proceed to deliberate over some important questions. For example, one question they faced was whether they would initiate joint philanthropy in the fourth generation, about ten of whom were already adults. The second and third generations had always done philanthropy separately, by branches. Another question was whether to start a private trust company to manage wealth for other high-net-worth families.

Unfortunately, what we hoped would become an ongoing engagement didn't last long. Although we know that they moved forward with respect to the foregoing issues, they accepted only limited follow-up from us. Kaye did subsequently facilitate the office's Mission Statement committee, whose work the whole family ratified. Hamilton continued to be a resource for the CEO. But we did not succeed in establishing a sufficient working alliance to leverage all that they had invested in our learning curve. Like some other families, they continue to bring various speakers in to each annual meeting (certainly a worthwhile thing to do) but have so far avoided tackling a major governance problem. We had hoped to lead them through an integrated, gradual, process of change. In retrospect, we fault ourselves for trying to take them too far, too fast. We overdid the content and underestimated the time it would take to let the ones who were comfortable with us serve as trust catalysts for the more reticent or apprehensive members of this very large family system.

We find that the bigger the family is, the more they resist formalizing an advisory team to provide on-going assistance. Cost cannot be claimed as a reason, as it might be with less wealthy families. Something else is at work. Unlike clinical therapy, in which the patient system feels both acute and chronic pain, and fears the consequences of failing to get help, the business systems we hear from often lack that awareness. They want to take little nibbles of consultation, but don't believe they need as much help as they do. Or perhaps they secretly do believe it. Awareness of the many layers and players in their drama may make them feel less threatened by isolated presenters than by a less controllable team with a long-term assignment. When we hear the question, "Why do we need more than one of you?" we have learned that the concern is not about money. It is about controlling the pace of change.

Be true to your team?

Differences among members of a consulting team are just as salient as those among the client family. Some differences are due to disciplinary perspectives. For example, technical advisors try to reduce uncertainty and provide solutions, while process advisors look for change through the family's own insight and dialectic. Attorneys are careful about rights, obligations, and compliance. Psychologists think about risk to the family's emotional fabric.

Other differences are matters of personality and working style. One of us has a greater need to plan our face-to-face meetings with groups—what we're going to say and who will do what. The other favors spontaneity: let's see what happens when we get in the room. But each of us will feel differently depending upon the clients and the task of the moment. Knowing each other well, and trusting each other to pursue or block an unplanned digression, is absolutely essential.

This means that the more work we do together, the better we are as a team. We can be on a conference call with one or more clients, without body language or other visual clues, yet still signal our thoughts to one another sufficiently to coordinate our interview or advising. The more the two of us work with a third colleague—an attorney, for example, or a philanthropy expert—and the longer we work with a client's existing advisors, the more comfortable all of us are. That, in turn, leads to a problem. How loyal should we be to one another? What if a family takes a dislike to one of us? The more people in the room, the more certain it is that some of them will be unhappy with at least one of the consultants, even after a productive session. And the less likely that they will say so at the time. It isn't our job to make all of them like all of us, all of the time. There are times when at least some members of the team have to be provocative. "Please all, and you please none," as Aesop said. For example, we may have to confront substance abuse, and a family's collusion in it.

On the one hand, we have said that the long-term changes financial families must make are best led by a consultant with broad, forward-looking vision. That person must form bonds with as many family members as possible, and definitely with their trust catalysts. He or she must also be a trust catalyst among the group of disparate outsiders. But if the leader has to be an advocate for a *fixed* team, in the long run it isn't going to work.

Sometimes, resistant clients will split the consultants: "You're helpful but your partner is not." This may be a pattern in their own dynamic that they would do well to look at, explore, and overcome. But it is also true that any of us may make a *faux pas*, or simply have a personal style that doesn't work well with particular clients. Should the team demonstrate loyalty—one for all and all for one—or should it demonstrate willingness to accommodate to this client system by replacing the miscast colleague? The answer is that teams should be neither too quick to dump a trusted colleague, nor too inflexible to consider doing so when it's in the best interests of the work.

The person who is team leader and principal liaison needn't always be the consultant whom the family first engaged. Nor does it matter whether it's the content expert or the process facilitator who performs this role. It needs to be whoever (1) can best advocate for the long-term process, to client members and especially to their leaders and trust catalysts; and (2) is in a position to respond to the clients in timely fashion and *proactively* stay in touch with them during periods of dormancy.

A content expert who has good rapport with family leaders has at least two things to fear when bringing in a family dynamics person as a co-consultant. One is that some or all family members who had been comfortable with the business/legal/financial consultation are suddenly uncomfortable with the suggestion that there may be something wrong with their family, mental health issues to be addressed, buried traumas to be exhumed. The other risk is that a good facilitator might lead the family to discuss issues and find resolutions at odds with the content expert's recommendations. They might decide the latter has been enjoying too much trust.

On the other hand, where a family therapist is the initial trusted consultant, bringing in a content expert can undermine the therapist's relationship with his clients. One of us learned this after he had worked for over a year with a sizeable international firm. Majority ownership was still with the founder, two of whose four children ran the company. This sister and brother had always been close since childhood, but they were battling for two different visions and styles of leadership. (Nor did they love each other's spouses.) They came up with various ideas about splitting ownership, each acquiring control of one corporation and serving as minority shareholder and director of the other's. The parents adamantly wanted them to keep the whole empire intact and "work together." However, they agreed to be introduced to one of the leading financial advisors to family firms.

We had a good meeting in the founder's office—both parents, both successors, the trusted family process consultant and the experienced, impressive financial expert. The latter stepped back from the successors' ideas about ways to divide the turf, to discuss what his firm would consider before making specific recommendations. He promised to get back to the founder with a suggested approach to the big picture, and did so soon thereafter. The initiating consultant was pleased with how the meeting had gone. Yet the parents not only rejected the idea of engaging the new firm, they soon ended the original engagement as well. The agenda had been to fix their warring children. The consultant had enjoyed their trust as long as they could believe he was only hypothetically entertaining the scenario of division. Bringing in a very knowledgeable, polished expert who might have offered some such solution went beyond the hypothetical, apparently, to the antithetical.

As we said earlier, well-designed exit strategies are vital for any kind of enterprise. Surely that aspect of teamwork is one which consultants should model, just as we model good communication, mutual respect, and our ability to disagree. The consulting team shouldn't rigidly stick together. Replace a team member, if necessary, to keep the work going forward. The consultants must then nurture and repair their own relationships, outside of the client system—just like a family.

Assuming that is the smart position to take, what strong relationships must be required to implement it! What self-confidence! The world of multidisciplinary consulting is not to be entered by the thin-skinned or the overly competitive. There will sometimes be as much work for a team to do behind the scenes, off the clock, as there is on the client's bill, especially in the course of their first five or ten cases together.

Conclusion

In addition to the three constant challenges, we have learned some things, and raised a problem to which there is no easy solution. The things we learned came from the literature cited in this article and from multidisciplinary study groups and consulting teams throughout the world, confirmed by our experience. They are:

• The alliance continues even when the process is slow and disappointing. The consultants may be the only ones who know it isn't over. Hold onto your notes, and make it easy for dormant clients to reach out to you when they wake up.

- Trust is itself a continuous process of building and testing. This is true in the client system, and the consultant system, and their intersection.

- It will not be possible for every member of a consulting team to form an alliance with every member of the client system. Therefore, the lead liaison has to be as much of a trust catalyst as possible to both groups.

Ultimately, though, commitment to the principle of multidisciplinary teams raises the paradox about loyalty. In any sport, teams perform better the more they play together. On the other hand, members of a consulting team have to be replaceable, within reason. Consequently, managing our own set of dynamic relationships, building and testing trust, always preserving the option of replacing players, yet somehow without demoralizing those on the bench, may prove to be the most difficult process challenge of all.

References

Alderfer, C.P. (1988). Understanding and consulting to family business boards. *Family Business Review, 1*(3), 249-261.

Barber, J., Hilburt-Davis, J., McKibbin, P., Swartz, S. & Wofford, J. (2002) Opportunities for multidisciplinary collaboration. *Proceedings*, Annual Conference, October 2002. Boston: Family Firm Institute

Barnes, L.B. (1981). Managing the paradox of organizational trust. *Harvard Business Review, 59,* 107-116.

Bork, D., Jaffe, D., Lane, S., Dashew, L. & Heisler, Q.G. (1995). *Working With Family Businesses*. San Francisco, CA: Jossey-Bass.

Bradach, J.L., & Eccles, R.G. (1989). Price, authority, and trust: From ideal types to plural forms. *Annual Review of Sociology, 15*, 97-118.

Davidow, T. & Narva, R. (2001) How multi-generational family firms transfer management control successfully. Based on a presentation to the Family Business Network, Rome. Needham, MA: Genus Resources, LLC.

Davis, P. (1983) Realizing the potential of the family business. *Organizational Dynamics, 12*(1), 47-56.

Grote, J. (2002). Multidisciplinary practices: emerging slowly…very slowly. *Journal of Financial Planning, 15*(4), 52-60.

Hamilton, S. & Kaye, K. (2003). The big dilemma for wealth creators: delegating. *Trusts and Estates,* May, 42-45.

Hilburt-Davis, J. & Senturia, P. (1995). Using the Process/Content Framework: Guidelines for the Content Expert. *Family Business Review, 8*(3), 189-199.

Hughes, J. (1997). *Family Wealth: Keeping it in the Family.* Princeton Junction, NJ: NetWrx, Inc.

Kaye, K. (1994). *Workplace Wars and How to End Them: Turning Personal Conflict into Productive Teamwork.* New York: AMACOM.

Kaye. K. (1995). How to rebuild business trust. *Family Business,* Summer, 27-31.

LaChapelle, K. & Barnes, L. (1998). The trust catalyst in family-owned businesses. *Family Business Review, 11*(1), 1-17.

Lansberg, I. (1999). *Succeeding generations.* Cambridge: Harvard University Press.

McCollom, M. (1992). The ownership trust and succession paralysis in the family business. *Family Business Review, 5*(2), 145-159.

Powell, W.W. (1987). Hybrid organizational arrangements. *California Management Review, 30,* 67-87.

Steier, L. (2001). Family firms, plural forms of governance, and the evolving role of trust. *Family Business Review, 14*(4), 353-367.

Swartz, S. (1989). The challenges of multidisciplinary consulting to family-owned businesses. *Family Business Review, 2*(4), 329-339.

Vago, M. (2003). "Outside" executives: coming in from the cold. *Proceedings,* Annual Conference, October 2003. Boston: Family Firm Institute

Whiteside, M. & Brown, F. (1991). Drawbacks of a dual systems approach to family firms: Can we expand our thinking? *Family Business Review, 4*(4), 383-395.

Afterword

ALTHOUGH PARTS of the foregoing articles may have challenged the reader by peeking into theoretical realms of developmental psychology, open systems, and family therapy—not to mention the requisite practical understanding of corporate governance, tax issues, trusts and estates—my most useful tools are quite simple. I rely on them all the time, like a carpenter's hammer and level, or a football coach's basic plays:

- Visualizing myself on a game plan from what I call Plan A, refocusing on shared goals, to more therapy-like interventions when necessary and when I've established sufficient alliance with the clients: Plan B, clarifying and classifying interpersonal differences; Plan C, testing their willingness to take individual leadership in changing; down to Plan D, analyzing chronic patterns of dysfunction; and if all else fails, Plan E, unilateral change, accepting that others won't change.

- Asking "what would happen if…" as many times as necessary until the "real" issues—the apprehensions a family has avoided talking about—get on the table.

- In Plan C, using the chart I call the "finger trap," because it blocks blamers from pointing their fingers at others. (Powerful medicine, isolating the family member who won't put anything in the section of the chart designating what he himself needs to change.)

- In Plan D, charting the conflict cycle.

- Explaining that there are at least three different kinds of trust—about honesty, about intentions, and about competence—and that trust is a process, not an absolute. Where one type has been lost, it may be possible to rebuild it gradually by using the type of trust that still exists, as a foundation.

- Refusing to assume that passing a business to the next generation, or passing wealth in tax-avoidant but personally restrictive ways, is the definition of success.

- Reminding clients that family success means the creation of opportunities for children beyond what their parents had, to actualize their own talents and proclivities.

- Joining the trust catalyst(s) in a family system, with whom an outside consultant must form a working relationship if he or she is to have influence within that family.

Any family-owned business can be approached on at least three different levels:

Acute crisis, or close-up lens. Often there's an acute, painful event or standoff, involving two or more individuals with specific grievances. They're eager, and at the same time afraid, to put those issues on the table.

Fundamentals, or wide-angle lens. Zooming out to the broadest questions, a consultant pushes the family business system to articulate its structure of family ownership and governance, including the shared vision, mission, two-to five-year goals, the ground rules on decision making, participation, and how members can pull out of the business relationship, if they choose, without ruining their family relationships. I compare these challenging deliberations to the work of Madison, Jefferson, and the other visionaries who framed our American Constitution.

Baggage, the middle ground. Somewhere in the middle, neither constitutional in nature nor an isolated challenge, are chronic sorts of issues such as poor patterns of communication, unresolved interpersonal resentments, lack of trust for one reason or another, a person stuck in a job he or she can't do well, false assumptions and expectations, or a major transition such as a death in the family or a looming retirement, for which mission statements and by-laws don't provide an adequate road map.

At which level does one begin? In the rare case (which I have yet to see) of a family that is experiencing no conflict but is merely looking for a facilitator-guide through a process of succession to the next generation, one would begin with the wide-angle lens. Let's understand and be sure we all mean the same thing by "our family business." Much as a nation's shared values, legal system, economic strengths and resource needs might guide its educational system, its foreign policy, or its choice of leaders, the shared business commitments of a family ought to guide its decisions about leadership transition.

In practice, however, when I've attempted to start there, to codify those broad shared agreements, the attempt soon exposes chronic issues of trust and other family baggage, which demand attention first.

The cases that begin in acute crisis over some very specific issue invariably arise from chronic problems at that middle level. Such a family is in no shape to start working on their mission statement or by-laws. Nor can the acute crisis be resolved without analyzing and confronting the baggage—the issues they have generally tried to ignore.

A mediator might help with an acute crisis, particularly if the goal is ending or reducing the business relationship as fairly and non-destructively as possible.

A family business generalist is well equipped to guide owners through the fundamentals of corporate governance and to share the best practices and common pitfalls of others who made similar transitions in similar circumstances. Together with the family's attorneys, the generalist can also formalize their by-laws, buy-sell agreements, incentive plans, and employee handbooks.

It's in that middle ground, however—the land of chronic miscommunication, distrust, grief, betrayal, rage, depression, addictions, tears, terrorism, intergenerational warfare, and old, old baggage—where the psychologist or family systems intervener is most needed and where we need to reach into the bag of tools listed above.

None of those insights or tools is original with me. Some I got from specific mentors, cited in these articles. Others I owe to basic philosophical tenets such as the oft-repeated, oft-forgotten, *money doesn't buy happiness*. Having known more than my share of individuals who control billions of dollars of net worth, I know how true that is. But money can, at least, employ wise advisors.

Index

The Author

Kenneth Kaye earned an A.B. in English literature (1966) and a Ph.D. in psychology and education (1970) from Harvard University. He was a Knox Fellow at the University of Cambridge, England. Later he trained in family therapy at the Family Institute of Chicago.

As a researcher, Dr. Kaye authored *The Mental and Social Life of Babies: How Parents Create Persons* and more than three dozen scientific articles on the first two years of human life. As a family therapist, he published *Family Rules: Raising Responsible Children*, as well as articles for *Psychology Today*, *Redbook*, *The Sciences*, *Family Business*, *Corporate Board*, *Nation's Business*, and many other magazines.

A faculty member at Northwestern University's Institute of Psychiatry, Kaye established his consulting specialty in 1986. The annual conference he founded on the Psychodynamics of Family Business has met annually since 1995. He is also a long-time Advisor Member and Consultant to Family Office Exchange (FOX).

An instrument-rated commercial pilot, Ken Kaye's work reflects diverse experiences including acting, sailing, tennis, and mountain climbing. He has four adult children, a daughter-in-law, and a first grandchild.

website: www.kaye.com

978-0-595-35708-6
0-595-35708-3